"STUD" OR  TAKE THE QUIZ

If your partner fails to climax, do you feel:

- Willing to help if you can?
- Guilty or partially responsible?
- That it's her problem and you can't be bothered with it?

Do you mentally compare your partner with other women?

- Not that I'm aware of.
- Sure, sometimes. Doesn't everyone?
- Yes, and I wish she'd lose weight/work out/curl her hair.

Which adjectives describe you as a lover?

- Giving, passionate, curious, and imaginative.
- Strong, long-lasting, a man of few words.
- Better than average, hornier than your normal guy.

While making love to a woman, do you ever tell her how wonderful she smells, how excited you are being with her, how good she feels, or how beautiful she is?

- Yes, frequently.
- I have in the past.
- No, I don't feel comfortable giving compliments.

The answers inside will tell you whether you're every woman's fantasy, challenge your beliefs about sex and women, and make you a more lovable lover in *and* out of bed.

DRIVE YOUR WOMAN WILD IN BED

A LOVER'S GUIDE TO SEX AND ROMANCE

STACI KEITH

WARNER BOOKS

A Time Warner Company

Warner Books, Inc., 1271 Avenue of the Americas,
New York, NY 10020

W A Time Warner Company

Printed in the United States of America

First Printing: December 1994

10 9 8 7 6

Library of Congress Cataloging-in-Publication Data

Keith, Staci.
  Drive your woman wild in bed : a lover's guide to sex and romance / Staci Keith.
    p.   cm.
  ISBN 0-446-67047-2
  1. Sex instruction for men. 2. Men—Sexual behavior. 3. Sexual excitement. 4. Sex in marriage. I. Title.
HQ36.K45   1994
613.9'52—dc20   94-15349
                                                                         CIP

Book design by Giorgetta Bell McRee
Cover design by Julia Kushnirsky
Cover photograph by Herman Estevez

To Scott Cole,
whose loving support
made this book possible

Contents

Acknowledgements

I would like to thank the countless hundreds whose interviews, both formal and informal, made this book possible. The candor and, yes, wit displayed by each and every one of you made my effort less a labor and more a love.

Let's Talk About Sex

Sex. It's not a simple issue, is it? Something that should be effortless, natural, and spontaneous has become mired down in anxiety and confusion. Or maybe it was always like that? Men say women are "bitches" and women say men are "pigs." Both misogyny and male-bashing are rampant throughout the culture. The hostility toward women is reflected in the patter of comedians, the voyeurism of music videos and bikini contests. Men are roundly abused in the self-help journals or portrayed as sadistic, lascivious jerks on tabloid TV. The message, however, is clear: sex is no less confusing than the way we feel about each other.

For women, the confusion is sometimes worse. Women haven't got the economic equality or the civil rights. They are often despised, ridiculed, and objectified. They are frequently the victims not only of violent crime but—more insidiously—double standards. Our culture breeds women with self-esteem problems, especially about their looks, instills impossible expectations of love and romance, then fails to tell them how to deal with their inevitable disappointment. Relationships, much to our surprise, are work! It isn't always "happily ever after" when we ride off into the sunset. All these factors conspire to make women difficult to understand—even to themselves.

I'm expounding on all this not just for your edification but to help you become an even *better* lover than you are already. Great lovers have three things in common: passion, sensitivity, and understanding. While I can improve your understanding, I can do little for your sensitivity or your passion. These are things I can only help you bring out in yourself. Understanding starts with putting yourself in somebody else's shoes—in this case, being more aware of how women feel about themselves.

By the end of this book you will have many tools at your disposal. If you use even half of them, you'll be a better lover than 98 percent of the men out there. *Great lovers are in short supply!* Even with new generations of sexual sophisticates, their numbers are dwindling.

Knowledge is power. It would be unconscionable for you to use the resources in this book to go out and ravage entire cheerleading squads or for the purpose of breaking hearts. You are in training to become an incredible, unforgettable, fantastic lover—not to set a new world record. I'm not here to govern the whims of your penis, but there are many sound reasons why you should EXERCISE CAUTION to avoid contracting some virulent illness that will put you permanently out of commission. Right? There are lots of nasty little diseases out there—the AIDS virus is only one.

In addition to viruses and such, you had better beware EMOTIONAL ILLNESSES. If a woman has an emotional illness centered around her sexuality, I don't care how great a lover you are, there's nothing you can do to make her better. If you happen to love a woman who is sexually dysfunctional, you need to evaluate how important sex is to you in the relationship. Can you do without terrific sex and not feel deprived? Underprivileged? Many otherwise wonderful relationships are not so wonderful in bed. As a society, we tend to place far too great an emphasis on sex. Sex is only one small part of living! There's also:

musicfoodcarssportstravelingworkclothesscience
familybeachesskydivingflirtingastrologybooks
ecologytelevisioneducationbeingalivepartiesba-
biestoolsculturecollegebuddieshistoryswimming
cookingSharperImagecataloguesfiscalplanningtalk-
ingShakespeareSundaysbeercomputersbeinghappy!

The following quotes are from some fine minds on the subject of sex:

"The position is ridiculous, the pleasure momentary, the expense damnable."

—Lord Chesterfield
English statesman (1694–1773)

"Love is two minutes, fifty-two seconds of squishing noises. It shows your mind isn't clicking right."

—Johnny Rotten

"When sex is good, it's 10 percent of a relationship; when sex is bad, it's 90 percent of a relationship."

—Michael Brooks
author, Instant Rapport

"When we can't have love, we settle for power."

> —*Ethel Person*
> *author,* Dreams of Love and Fateful Encounters

"You think intercourse is a private act; it's not, it's a social act. Men are sexually predatory in life; and women are sexually manipulative. When two individuals come together and leave their gender outside the bedroom door, then they make love. If they take it inside with them, they do something else, because society is in the room with them."

> —*Andrea Dworkin*
> *author,* Fire and Ice, *etc.*

Wise words, indeed.

DRIVE YOUR WOMAN WILD IN BED

1

Studly or Dudly . . . ?
(A Quiz)

TESTING YOUR SEXUAL AND EMOTIONAL SOPHISTICATION

1. During sex, if your partner gives you a suggestion, do you feel:
   A. Receptive.
   B. Anxious.
   C. Angry/Impatient.

2. Do you have trouble being spontaneous? If your partner wanted to pull over in the car and make love, would you do it?
   A. Very possibly.
   B. It's doubtful.
   C. Never.

3. If your partner fails to climax, do you feel:
   A. Willing to help her if you can.
   B. Guilty or partially responsible.
   C. It's her problem and you can't be bothered with it.

4. Have you been accused by three or more women of not being affectionate? Of not hugging and kissing as much as they'd like?
   A. Never.
   B. Once or twice.
   C. All the time.

5. Do you have trouble being mentally, physically, and emotionally "in the moment"? Do you worry or allow your mind to wander on irrelevant things while making love?
   A. No.
   B. Sometimes.
   C. Often.

6. Do you neglect your appearance and/or your hygiene? Do you need to clean your nails, brush your teeth, bathe, shave, or trim your facial hair?
   A. No, I'm pretty diligent about things like that.
   B. I've been a little slack lately.
   C. If she really loves me it won't matter.

7. Is oral sex your number one priority? If so, do you ever pressure your partner into performing oral sex on you?
   A. I like it but it's not as fulfilling as intercourse.
   B. Sometimes I lose patience and yell at her for being so uptight.
   C. It's all I think about and if a woman doesn't fellate me, I just go out and find someone who will.

8. Do you watch television, especially sports programs, during most of your free time?
   A. Occasionally.

B. More than I probably should.
C. As often as possible.

9. Do you have any close friends of the same sex?
   A. Yes.
   B. One.
   C. No one I feel especially close to.

10. Do you have any friends who are women?
    A. Yes, several.
    B. I am acquainted with some women.
    C. No, none.

11. Do you masturbate to pornographic materials or films?
    A. I have but I don't make a regular habit of it.
    B. Sometimes.
    C. Regularly.

12. Do you mentally (and unfavorably) compare your partner with other women or women you see in magazines or on TV?
    A. Not that I'm aware of.
    B. Sure, sometimes—doesn't everybody?
    C. Yes, and I wish she'd lose weight/work out/curl her hair/wear heels, etc.

13. Secretly, do you feel dirty or unattractive?
    A. No.
    B. Only sometimes, but when I do, it's very strong.
    C. Yes, most of the time.

14. Are you frequently angry or critical of your partner? Do you believe you're doing her a favor by telling her certain truths about herself?

A. No.

B. Yes, she really makes me mad sometimes.

C. It's the only way I can get my point across.

15. Has anyone ever accused you of being a workaholic?

    A. I work hard but I'm home most nights.

    B. I get a little manic about work, especially when an important project comes up.

    C. Yes, but it's better to be a workaholic than an alcoholic.

16. When's the last time you brought your Significant Other a surprise bouquet/card/bottle of perfume?

    A. This month.

    B. In the last six months.

    C. We feel those kinds of empty gestures are unnecessary in our relationship.

17. When having an orgasm, do you say anything or allow yourself to vocalize in any way?

    A. Yes, I exuberantly express myself (except when others might hear).

    B. Occasionally, but it embarrasses me.

    C. Never. I feel too stupid.

18. When's the last time you spontaneously hugged, kissed, or told your partner you loved her?

    A. Today, yesterday, or the day before.

    B. A couple of weeks ago.

    C. I show her in so many other ways how I feel about her that she doesn't need to hear me say it.

19. How often do you go out with the guys?

    A. Once every one or two weeks. We don't have a set time.

    B. A set time every week—no matter what
       (Saturday night poker games, for instance).
    C. A lot—hey, it's the guys, right?

20. How often do you compliment your partner on her
    appearance?
    A. Often. She looks wonderful to me.
    B. When she gets all dolled up, I'll occasionally say
       something.
    C. Never. She doesn't keep herself up the way I
       would like her to. *Or:* she's good-looking enough
       without my giving her a swelled head.

21. In social situations or at restaurants with your
    partner, do you let your eyes wander over every
    attractive woman you see?
    A. No. I try to be conscientious about my partner. I
       want her to feel comfortable with me—not
       offended and insecure.
    B. Sure, I sneak a peek when no one's looking.
    C. Yes. After all, what am I supposed to do? Put
       blinders on?

22. Which of the following do you consider the
    masculine ideal?
    A. A man who's affectionate and considerate, but
       doesn't allow himself to get railroaded. Maybe
       he's not a god, but he keeps himself up. He can
       talk to his partner about feelings without
       choking.
    B. A man who doesn't cheat on, hit, or bankrupt
       his partner. He knows his role and she knows
       hers.
    C. A really rich guy with a yacht and a twelve-inch
       penis. I know that's what women want because I

see so many women flocking around guys like
that.

23. Which of the following do you consider *romantic?*
    A. That scene in *Out of Africa* where Robert Redford
       washes Meryl Streep's hair.
    B. That scene in *Risky Business* where Tom Cruise
       bends Rebecca De Mornay over the couch.
    C. That scene in *9 1/2 Weeks* where Mickey Rourke
       watches Kim Basinger do a really sexy strip show.

24. Which adjectives best describe you as a lover?
    A. Giving, passionate, curious, and imaginative.
    B. Strong, long-lasting, a man of few words.
    C. Better-than-averagely endowed. Hornier than
       your normal guy. I always have an erection.

25. How would you describe your father?
    A. A warm, supportive man.
    B. Mr. Personality but we didn't see much of him.
    C. A jerk.

26. How long do you spend on foreplay before
    penetration?
    A. Ten minutes or more.
    B. Two to five minutes.
    C. We don't really need foreplay. She has an orgasm
       regardless. *Or:* we understand that I'm the one
       who needs sex.

27. Do you believe you are 100 percent responsible for
    a woman's orgasm?
    A. No, not 100 percent—50 percent, maybe.
    B. Yes. She can't have one unless I know how to
       turn her on.

C. No, that's her business. If women weren't so uptight, they'd have more orgasms.

28. What answer best describes women?
    A. Thinking, feeling human beings with strengths and weaknesses like all the rest of us. It must be hard to be globally regarded as a second-class citizen.
    B. Moody and complex, but I definitely need them. Sometimes I can't help blaming women for staying in abusive relationships or allowing themselves to be sexually abused as children.
    C. Basically, you've got your good women and you've got your bad women. Good women don't drink, do drugs, or sleep around. They stand by their men no matter what. Bad women use a man up and then spit him out. They lie to you, cheat on you, spend your money, and nag you to death. I wish women weren't so damn angry all the time.

29. Would you fly in an airplane piloted by a woman?
    A. Definitely.
    B. I think I'd be a little nervous.
    C. No way. They can't drive a car so why should I expect them to safely pilot a plane?

30. While making love to a woman, do you ever tell her how wonderful she smells, how excited you are being with her, how good she feels or how beautiful she is?
    A. Yes, frequently.
    B. I have in the past.
    C. No, I don't feel comfortable giving compliments.

After completing this test, put your A answers, B answers, and C answers into three separate columns. If you find yourself stumped between two answers, place both answers into their appropriate columns. Be honest!

1. If you have a majority of C answers:

You will be challenged to change erroneous beliefs about sex, women, even yourself. C answers don't expose your worthlessness; they merely signal a problem with relating to others. You may have been accused of being an angry, difficult, or moody person and probably have a background of physical battery, alcoholism, or other dysfunction. You gravitate toward young, meek, or compliant women and enjoy the company of other men more than that of women. You're rarely graceful under pressure. Your fuse is notoriously short. There's a chance you have an ingestive disorder as well—overeating, overdrinking, or taking drugs.

One of the biggest difficulties facing men nowadays is finding the right way to define their masculinity. Gone are the days when men worked and women stayed home. Today, two incomes are not a plus, they're a necessity. If women give birth *and* provide for the family, where does that leave men? Their "sole provider" role is being challenged on all sides. Being a man means moving beyond the quest for alpha male status (having others be subordinate to you). There is no war between the sexes unless you enter the fray. Please rethink some of your attitudes concerning women and concerning yourself. Seek counseling, if necessary. If you don't, you run the risk of poisoning every relationship you have.

2. If you have a majority of B answers:

Some of the B options were extremely subtle, as subtle perhaps as your confused, less-than-positive (or unrealistically positive) feelings about women. If you had a preponderance of B answers, it's likely you've survived at least one stormy relationship. Your level of dysfunction may not be severe, but it can be problematic. You sometimes have trouble seeing women for who they really are instead of who you'd like them to be. Moreover, it's difficult to view them as people—to you, they are or are not possible sexual partners. You're not terribly close to any member of your family (or, alternately, very involved with your mother). You may feel a strong sense of isolation. When you do fall in love, you fear losing control or being made to look like a fool.

Having a healthy relationship requires something more than a frame of negative references (see for example Question 22, answer B: "A man who doesn't cheat on, hit, or bankrupt his partner"). It requires active involvement. Too often men "achieve" a relationship, then expect it to be there with little or no additional effort on their part. In a relationship, you never hit the end zone and spike the ball. You're always playing the game. That's why you can't neglect, ignore, or cease to woo the woman who loves you. After a while, she *will* go somewhere else. To increase your understanding of women and their feelings, try talking to them, not necessarily about sex, but about experiences, emotions . . . life. Be sure to listen. Read all you can about women. Knowledge—not a big penis—is power.

3. If you have a majority of A answers:

Congratulations! You scored high on the stud-o-meter.
And if you had all A answers, you're every woman's fantasy. Chances are you feel pretty good about yourself
and have a healthy respect for women. You neither deify
nor denigrate them. They're "thinking, feeling human
beings" just like you.

It's doubtful that you brag about your sexual exploits
or accomplishments, nor do you feel complacent about
your abilities as a lover. You're not naive—you suspect
that women who overdramatize their sexuality have
identity problems; they're not just "hot babes trolling
for man meat." You've had good, solid, happy relationships. If a relationship did end, you remained on speaking terms with your girlfriend.

The more A answers you logged, the greater the likelihood your parents had a peaceful and harmonious relationship themselves. We pattern what we see.

Note: Whether you had A, B, or C answers, there are
still many things you will learn by reading *Drive Your
Woman Wild in Bed*!

2

The Two Greatest Sexual Secrets of All Time

Ask a woman today what single quality she thinks most men are lacking in bed and she'll probably say "passion." "Lack of imagination" will run a close second. Passion is the key to everything. Whether it's passion about your work, passion about being a good father—whatever. Sexually, it's what distinguishes the men from the boys.

Secret #1: Passionate men aren't afraid to make noise during sex. Passionate men make love like they've got one day to live and they take no prisoners. Passion is not necessarily tender. Sometimes it's crude and barbaric and exciting and dangerous. Passion (the first of two great sexual secrets) is contagious and completely uninhibited.

Webster's defines the verb "ravish" as "to transport with joy or ecstasy," and the adjective "ravishing" as "delightful; entrancing."

Secret #2: Ravish is a close cousin to passion. It is women's number one sexual fantasy. *Ravish, incidentally, has nothing to do with rape.* Rape is nonconsensual sex. Rape is when you persist after she says no. Ravish is when you look at your wife of fifteen years and are seized with a sudden voracious hunger for her. Ravish is when you are so overcome by her beauty and desirability you can't help it, you tackle her right there on the living room carpet and have unspeakable congress. Women's romance novels are full of ravish. With ravish there's an unspoken surrender on her part and wild-eyed desire on yours. With ravish you get rumpled clothes and a death-defying EKG. Ravish isn't pink, it's scarlet and black and electric blue.

Ravish is an attitude.

The goddess in every woman wants to believe you are so overwhelmed with desire for her, you're driven to dark and desperate deeds. Ravish, interestingly enough, requires no foreplay. It's immediate and consuming and completely in the moment. Tap into your raw, primordial passion. The secret to being passionate is being completely in the moment. That means not judging what you did the moment before or planning what you should do the next moment. If you, too, want to join the ranks of the legendary lovers, you will open yourself up to the passion within you. Knowing someone is passionate about being sexual with you is the greatest turn-on a woman can know.

3

Women's Secret Secrets/Women's Secret Fears

During the many lectures I have given, I always ask men in the audience to tell me about their most unforgettable lover, and their answers are specific. Rarely do the words "big boobs" or "gives head" arise. The ribbon consistently went to the woman who managed to convey—openly or subtly—that *he* was the best lover that *she* had ever had. It seemed that being good in bed had less to do with what she did for his body than what she did for his ego.

With women, it's a little different. They want *you* to want *them* more than you've wanted anyone in the history of the world. Again, that maddening fairy-tale princess mentality creeps in! Because every woman is a goddess inside. No—every woman is *the* goddess inside. No matter if she is four hundred fifty pounds, bald, and wears a pith helmet, every woman wants that goddess paid tribute. That's why women melt over those traditional emblems of worship—roses, poetry, gifts: they're an offering on the shrine of their womanhood.

Woe betide you if you provoke the ire of your personal goddess! Remember the time you were out together and an attractive woman passed? You're looking at the woman and your goddess is looking at you. Why? a) to see if you were drooling; and b) to smack you if you were. Case in point: you and your partner are watching TV. Your partner (innocently, it seems) asks you if you find this or that actress attractive. You, blundering, say, "Yeah, she's a babe!" Later, when you ask your partner to get you a beer, she stomps her foot and shouts, "Well, why don't you get that babe to do it!" You see? Respect must be paid to the goddess inside every woman. Should women be this testy? Probably not. But the fact is, most are. *Whether they admit it or not.*

And you don't like your partner looking at other men any more than she likes you looking at women. Now, I'm not suggesting you poke your eyes out with two hot sticks. I'm merely telling you that half a woman's sexual happiness is her sexual trust. When you're out together, keep your eyes to yourself. When you're out with your buddies, feel free to make Slinkee-eyes at every woman alive. It's a respect issue more than anything. Being respectful to your partner doesn't mean you're less of a man or that you're being led around by the short hairs.

In other words, your partner doesn't need to know who you find attractive—unless you get some kind of sick thrill out of making her feel angry and insecure. And turnabout is *not* fair play, either. It seems that every time you hear a woman squealing about some cute movie actor, there's a disgruntled husband muttering, "Oh, yeah? I happen to know he's gay!"

Legendary lovers know that great sex is letting go of fear and insecurity. If you're having problems, your partner may fear any of the following and it may be affecting your sexual relationship together:

- Losing you to another woman
- Losing you to fantasies of another woman

- Getting older
- Getting pregnant
- Your accidentally hurting her during intercourse
- Not being a good enough: mother
                              wife
                              lover
                              cook
                              breadwinner
- Not being pretty enough

By comparison, men's fears are a little different:

- Not being able to provide for the family
- Not having a big enough penis/not being a good lover
- Having another man sleep with his partner
- People thinking he is dominated by his partner
- Being homosexual

The common denominator, of course, is that we don't measure up.

4

The Myth of Manly Men

Misconception number one is that men want (and need) sex all the time or they'll die. The truth is, we're all different and we all have different needs. For most people, sexual appetites are seasonal: sometimes they want a lot, sometimes not as much. Sex is always an obsession when you're not getting enough of it! In a relationship, sex is the same way. There will be times when you make love twice a day and times when you're lucky to make love twice a month. That's *de rigueur* in any relationship when kids and work, taxes and in-laws, conspire to dampen ardor.

Misconception number two is that a woman is either a saint or a slut. That's why there are men who marry a sexually inhibited woman, bitch about how uptight she is, and use that to justify their numerous liaisons with sexually uninhibited women. Saint-and-slut. Commonly, they think a "frigid" woman doesn't like sex so she won't cheat on them, whereas a woman with a healthy sexual appetite will be pawing delivery boys and pizza carriers as soon as their back is turned. This, in addition to being representative of a troglodyte mentality, is erroneous. It's the sexually unsatisfied woman who will eventually cheat, not the woman who knows what she wants in bed. One problem here is that since many women blossom sexually later in life than most men, the shy young virgin you married at twenty-one may acquire appetites you never dreamed of at thirty-eight. And a woman's sexual capacities can be enormous.

Misconception number three (a close cousin of number two) is that a man should marry a woman he respects and sleep with women he doesn't—prostitutes, "bimbos," "sleazes." We have a classic sexual archetype in this culture (Marilyn Monroe embodies it perfectly) of a "dumb blonde with big breasts." Is stupidity inherently sexy? No, probably not. But a stupid woman isn't a woman you'll ever run the risk of *respecting*. It is this aspect of men's sexual psychology that feminists deplore—not the existence of sexy women.

Misconception number four is that if you provide a decent income, don't drink too much, cheat on or beat your Significant Other, that makes you a perfect partner. This isn't true, either. These things should be a given in a relationship—on both sides. One happy philosophical gentleman I interviewed said it this way: "You can't watch sports all day, wolf your dinner down without any conversation, and watch sports all night and expect it to work out. It won't."

He's right.

5

Q & A

Dear Staci:

I'm so mad I could spit. Do nice guys always finish last? I'm constantly playing second fiddle to some butthead or offering a shoulder for women to cry on who've had their hearts broken three million times by the same jerk while I get overlooked. I hate it. Why doesn't nice play well with the ladies?

Walter L., Chicago, Illinois

Dear Walter:

Nice *does* play well with the ladies. The problem is, nice guys (like yourself, for instance) invariably pick the worst women! Women who are so hung up in one dysfunctional relationship after another that there's little chance they'll ever see how sweet, warm, and wonderful life with you could be. A great many "nice guys," however, are more in love with their whole romantic scenario ("I love her but she treats me so bad") than they are the actual object of their affections! It's like a real-life enactment of country-western lyrics. Ultimately the "nice guy" has just as much trouble with intimacy as the women he covets: it's just manifested in a different way.

Walter, my advice is this: stop making yourself available to these women and start making yourself available to yourself. Take up a hobby or join a class. Stop filling those empty hours with shallow women. As you broaden your horizons, not only will you feel better about yourself, you'll dwell less obsessively on women who don't love you and quite possibly find one who does. You may reasonably expect a little backsliding but don't let that deter you from your goal.

Dear Staci:

I'm a really nice guy and not bad-looking but when I get around members of the opposite sex (especially attractive ones) I become completely tongue-tied. It's like stage fright, I'm so nervous! I'd do anything to be less of a dork around women. Can you help me?

Marv W., Los Cerritos, California

Dear Marv:

I'll tell you what helped me: acting lessons! Of course for the first six weeks of class I was incapable of uttering a word. Then I slowly came out of hibernation and before long I was performing whole monologues. When we can achieve something even more daunting than talking to an attractive woman (such as performing in front of an entire class), the rest is easy! Now I lecture for three hours at a stretch across the country—sometimes in front of TV cameras—and I give all the credit to the acting lessons I suffered through. Even so, you can expect a certain degree of nervousness when conversing with a sexy woman. After all, that's to be expected! Eleanor Roosevelt, that wisest of souls, once remarked: "You must do the thing you think you cannot

do," and if you live your life by that, Marv, there will be
no stopping you.

With or without acting lessons, Marv, you *can* learn to
overcome your fear of rejection.

The cat chases the mouse. The mouse may twitch her
whiskers beguilingly, she may even invite you to dinner,
but nine times out of ten, you'll be the one making the
first move.

Strangely enough, many less-than-average-looking
men show the most moxie in asking women out. No
matter how awesome the babe, they approach un-
daunted, possessed of one simple truth: it's a numbers
game. If they ask fifty women out, one, two—maybe
ten—will accept. They know it's a numbers game and
now you know it, too. The trouble is getting enough
nerve to play the game in the first place.

It's an odd exercise I'm asking you to do but if you
want to cure yourself of that wicked stage fright, you
must do it. First:

1. Get a blank sheet of paper and a pen.
2. Visualize yourself approaching the object of your
   heart's desire.
3. Now think of the worst possible consequence of
   your proposing a date (she points, laughs, calls you
   a jerk, tells her friends, whatever).
4. Write down each horrible scenario and *read it out
   loud*.

When you verbalize your fears, when you see them on
paper, you go a long way toward overcoming them. They
can only have a death grip on your courage when you
allow them to rattle around in your head like so many
dried peas. Beautiful women are especially intimidating,
but don't you think they intimidate everyone? That's

why so many lovely ladies are home alone on Saturday night.

You must do it—if for no other reason than to prove to yourself that you can.

What's the best way to ask a woman out? Directly. Most men stare at their shoes and mumble, "Would you like to go out sometime?" Be specific! Say, "Hey, I just won two tickets to the Save the Squirrels concert. I'd really like it if you went with me." Depending on how well you know the woman, sometimes it's better to suggest lunch or an afternoon activity. Evening dates can be a little heavy.

Your looks are obviously her first impression of you, but there is every chance she's going to say yes. Why? You will learn how to approach her (Chapter 6), you're dressing for sex-cess (Chapter 7), while you've already gained the confidence that comes from understanding women and how they think (Chapter 3). If, however, she tells you something other than yes, here's how to read it:

"Maybe sometime."	Means: no
"I've got a boyfriend."	Means: no
"I've been real busy lately."	Means: no
"I'll call you sometime."	Means: no
"I'm not dating at all right now."	Means: no
"I'm a lesbian."	Means: no
"You're really nice, but . . ."	Means: no

The other secret about overcoming the fear of rejection is knowing when not to take that rejection personally. Often—quite often—when a woman says no she simply hasn't had enough time to consider what her feelings are. She feels pressured to give you an answer right away. Today, women have an extraordinary need for caution. How does she know you're not a date-rapist, child molester, or axe-murderer? It's best to invest some time in getting to know her before you ask her out, because that way she'll feel more comfortable with you. This benefits you as well. After all, what man wants to drop fifty dollars on drinks and dinner only to discover the woman of his dreams is really an ex-mechanic from Brooklyn named Joe?

I do not encourage you to rehearse any imaginary dialogue in front of the mirror. It would be painful for you to watch, and it just sets a woman's teeth on edge to have you lay some slicked-up line on her. Far better for you to fly by the seat of your pants even if you *do* fumble (fumbling can be endearing). Do appreciate her as a woman, yes, but see her as a human being first. She's just as nervous talking to you as you are to her. Awkwardness can be expected. Because I can guarantee that her biggest concern is how not to appear to be so big a ditz that you change your mind about asking her out.

A male friend of mine put it this way: "They can send a man to the moon. Am I so yellow-bellied I can't hitch up my underwear, paste a smile on my face, and ask a woman out on a date?"

The ball's in your court, Marv.

Dear Staci:

There's this girl I really like. We hang out all the time, I take her places, pay for things, but whenever I make my move, she tells me she just wants to be friends. Is she blowing me off, or what?
                                Miguel I., Santa Monica, California

Dear Miguel:

Ah, yes, the old "friends" gambit! Some people are so good at playing that game! Loosely translated, this means "I like you fine, I like the attention, but I'm not attracted enough to you to have sex with you." Trust me, it bites. What to do? Well, Miguel, it's time for a gut check. Do you like her enough to "just be friends"? That means putting a harness on those hormones, bub. Because she ain't gonna change. What might change, however, is you. If you start going out with other girls not only will you possibly find a woman with whom you have chemistry, your "friend" might come to the party. Under no circumstances, however, do I advise you to date other women for the sole purpose of making her jealous. And whatever you do, don't lie and say you're dating (we can smell this old ploy faster than a hound dog can sniff up a hoofprint). Don't even make a point of telling her you're dating when you really are. Let her find out. If she still isn't interested, chalk it up as one of life's experiences. If she is interested, you might ask yourself: "Is it me she wants or my undivided attention?" Food for thought, hmmm?

6

Women: Where to Find Them/What to Do When You Have

HOW TO MEET WOMEN

In the most ludicrous mating ritual of the animal kingdom, we humans contrive—and I mean contrive—to meet each other. Literature is full of the lovesick scheming to insinuate themselves with the beloved. They've cross-dressed *(As You Like It)*, traveled great distance *(Romeo and Juliet)*, only to ultimately and sometimes triumphantly kill themselves *(Antony and Cleopatra,* Tolstoy's *Anna Karenina,* Flaubert's *Madame Bovary,* Zola's *Nana,* Wharton's *The House of Mirth* . . . you get my idea). Surely there must be an easier way to accomplish the very basic task of pairing off.

Once upon a time, partners were assigned to us like so many bunkmates. Marriages were 95 percent financial and 5 percent compatible. Love was a stealthy, backstairs arrangement often resulting in debt and illegitimate children. Charles II of England (among countless other monarchs) fathered well over twenty children out of wedlock and ran his country into the ground trying to finance them all. My point is, modern ways, however flawed, are still the best.

The mating crisis is exacerbated by a woman's (somewhat annoying) propensity to sit and wait for you to find her—princesses all, dainty feet extended. Even dating services have trouble keeping women enrolled (60 to 65 percent of all members at Great Expectations, the nation's largest dating service, are men). So what's a nice, friendly *lonely* guy to do? Let's examine your options:

BARS: includes nightclubs, discos, restaurants with bars; anywhere liquor is served.

<u>Pros:</u> If variety is the spice of life, then bars are so spicy they'll give you heartburn. They do afford you ample opportunity to "scope out the talent" before singling out a woman to approach. Bars can build your confidence or blast your ego so it behooves you to cultivate thickness of skin, good taste, the right timing, witty repartee, and a handsome appearance. If, by chance, you get shot out of the saddle, there are always plenty of others to choose from. The odds improve considerably the more women you approach.

<u>Cons:</u> Women in bars are—and are not—available. The problem stems primarily from a difference in agendas. Most men aren't there to find a wife or even a girlfriend. Most men are there to get laid. Many women, on the other hand, go to bars just to flirt, and since bars are superficial environments (meaning everyone is being evaluated on how he/she looks), you're going to be judged superficially, too (how tall? how handsome? how rich? how available?). Know going in that the sexuality some women use to get your attention is all smoke and mirrors. Don't be deceived by the tight skirts and half-

bare bosoms. It isn't always, or even usually, an invitation to have sex. Most women dress sexy because it makes them feel desirable—*not* to get pinched, grabbed, propositioned, leered at, laughed at, or treated like a prostitute. Remember also the beer you drank that made you so eloquent in the bar may fail you in bed. Impotence is a close cousin of alcohol. Remember, though, if a sexual encounter occurs you absolutely *must* wear a condom and you cannot drive home afterward (if you're drunk) or make her drive home (if she's drunk). A wise man realizes that a lot of women use sex to get closer, to establish intimacy, while a lot of men—yourself included, perhaps—are having sex to have sex. With this in mind, do not treat this woman like a disposable condom post-coitus. In a social environment like a bar, word *does* travel.

DATING SERVICES: includes video dating, where you view videotapes and read profiles; matchmaking services, where you are matched with people based on certain criteria; photo dating, where pictures and profiles are presented and selections are made through a mediator.

<u>Pros:</u> The messages you get at a dating service are much less confusing than those you get at a bar. It's clean and crisp, direct yet impersonal—you never have to ask a woman out face-to-face. Rejections (should any be forthcoming) are handled in the same brisk, efficient manner: the service contacts you with a yes or no, depending. Video dating (arguably your best bet of these options) lets you decide who you want to go out with. On the other hand, matchmaking services will, based on a battery of compatibility tests, choose your dates for you.

Since appearance factors into sexual chemistry, with video dating you are able to view, in the relative privacy of a cubicle, prospective dates, hear what they have to say, and read what they tell you about themselves in their profiles. Busy at the office? While most memberships have time limitations, you're free to make selections when your schedule permits. You also get a lot of valuable information up front—stuff that's socially hazardous to ask (does she smoke? have kids? has she ever been married? is she legally separated? will she divorce soon?).

<u>Cons:</u> Dating services, like insurance companies, are *not* not-for-profit organizations. They can be pricey—sometimes $2,000 and more. That means missing out on a lot of warm, intelligent, love-rich but pocket-poor women you might otherwise meet. There's the disparity of men-to-women percentages to consider, too, leading many dating services to offer drastically reduced membership prices to get more women to join. Then there's the stigma of "having to go to a dating service to find a date" to be gotten over. Be aware that dating services will admit anyone, so don't expect every woman you meet to have been effectively screened no matter what the salesperson tells you. The possibility still exists that she's married, infected, just out of prison, or has twenty kids when she claims to have none. So go in with your eyes open.

PARTIES: includes formal and informal functions, picnics, art gallery openings, any social gathering of friends or strangers.

<u>Pros:</u> The more people you know, the better your chances of being introduced to somebody wonderful. Don't be afraid to put the word out (wives and girl-

friends of close friends make the most diligent match-makers). Force yourself to talk to anyone who seems interesting, including other men. Men have friends and sisters and cousins. Your main objective is to have *fun* at the party, not to pant and leer like a sailor on shore leave. Don't kid yourself that women don't have wolf radar—they do. The easiest way to camouflage your sexual hunger is to dispense with it entirely. Don't think you can put it in a costume. Change your objective and your attitude. You're at the party to have fun and make friends. Anything sexual is incidental entertainment.

Why not make it easy on yourself? Have someone else do all the work for you! You see her. She's lovely. Watch her and observe who she speaks with. When a male member of her group makes a move for the punch bowl, introduce yourself to him, apologize for being so presumptuous, then ask to be introduced to that absolutely ravishing woman. You're direct without being confrontational, oblique but not conniving. The presence of others makes you less intimidating and relieves the pressure of having to think of something brilliant to say. Introductions are charming. They hark back to a more chivalrous and respectful age. No woman wants some strange man sidling up to her with a look and a line. Lines went out with platform shoes in the 1970s.

<u>Cons:</u> Even the most aggressively handsome and confident extrovert has moments of doubt. He falters, wondering, "Can I do this?" Parties can be agonizing for all of us. Despite our best efforts to sound witty, conversations lag, the sublime degenerates into the trivial, someone's always handsomer or wealthier or has more hair. Sometimes we drink to overcome our shyness only to end up clutching the porcelain in some upstairs bathroom. Ah, yes, the joys of social engagements!

THE GROCERY STORE: encompasses any retail outlet or public place where men and women congregate.

Pros: Women shop. Armed with checkbook and credit card, they descend *en masse* to find the perfect shoe, the perfect dress, the perfect yogurt. Gourmet items by the boatload. A discerning man can tell a lot about a woman by the food she has in her grocery cart (married? single? kids? cats? dogs?). He can strike up a conversation with her in the soup aisle.

Be honest about your reasons for approaching her—within reason. Within reason precludes "because you have big hooters" and other such indelicacies. Honest goes something like:

> "I feel like the biggest jerk coming over here. I don't know you and I guess you can tell I'm not very good at this, but I'd kick myself for the rest of my life if I didn't say hi."

Or . . .

> "For the last ten minutes I've been daring myself to say hi. I thought I'd feel like a real jerk but now, talking to you, it's a lot easier than I ever would have imagined."

If she's receptive, chat briefly and move on. *Do not ask her out.* Give her time to finish her shopping, then approach her again once she's had a chance to: 1) get over the initial shock; 2) cultivate a rabid curiosity about you; 3) warm to your romantic possibilities. Never, absolutely never, act slick or cool. You'll come off looking like you do this all the time. The more genuinely abashed and awkward you are, the better. When you in-

vite her out for coffee, ask for her work number and
offer to give her yours. If you want, you can give her
both your work and your home numbers as a show of
trust and credibility.

Cons: When approaching a woman in a public place remember you are strangers to each other. It's a little
scary for her to talk to someone she doesn't know. You
are faced with the bleak prospect of initiating conversation. Realize that any move you make will be suspect
and your motives for doing so transparent as water.
Don't attempt a pretence of casualness (I casually bump
my cart against yours, I casually apologize, I casually ask
your opinion on different brands of butter).

BLIND DATES: includes dates with people your
friends have previously introduced you to; any "fix-ups."

Pros: Women you can meet in single's bars. Interesting,
stimulating women you will meet through friends. Make
as many friends as you can—male and female. Friends
have friends and sisters and cousins, any of whom you'll
be introduced to if you so desire. The absolute best way
to meet a woman is to be introduced to her. A lot of
women are afraid to go out with men they don't know
or don't have acquaintances in common with.
   Meeting through friends is probably the best way of
finding a Significant Other. You can't frighten her off
because you've been "preapproved" by mutual acquaintances. If the axiom "Birds of a feather flock together"
holds true, you'll automatically have things in common.
If there's any initial awkwardness, rest assured she's feeling it, too. Once again, I exhort you to be honest—hon-
esty is very disarming! A well-timed . . .

"Boy, I was nervous coming over here!"

Or . . .

"I felt weird going out on a blind date. I kept expecting some kind of Woody Allen nightmare-date-from-hell story but so far I haven't slobbered on myself or put an eye out. I guess I'm doing pretty good."

The blind date jitters are universal. Right away you'll be on common ground. Remember: whenever a man speaks candidly about his feelings, most women warmly respond.

<u>Cons:</u> For obvious reasons if you're going on a blind date, don't fantasize about what you were told your date might look like. If you find her attractive, say so. If she's absolutely the last woman on earth you'd consider being with, make a short night of it and go home. *Do not tell a woman you're going to call when you have no intention of doing so.* It's cruel. A polite "Thanks for the terrific evening" will suffice.

IN SEARCH OF'S: includes all advertisements or listings for singles wanting to meet other singles.

Example:

DWF, fit, fun, and fabulous. I like Beethoven, Courvoisier, and spontaneous trips to the beach. You are between 35-50, responsible without being humorless. D or WM, possibly with grown or near-grown children (white horse optional). If I unbraid my golden tresses, will you climb up? Serious contenders only.

<u>Pros:</u> Who can resist reading the ISOs? Who hasn't wondered what might happen if she/he published an

ISO of her/his own? There's an element of mystery and intrigue you won't get on a blind date.

Not everyone is 100 percent honest about what she/he looks like, so to avoid any misunderstandings, some ISOers specify what they're looking for (weight, hair color, age, etc.). But several successful ISO couples I know urge you to keep an open mind. "You never know what you're looking for until you find it," says David B., who met Tammy, now his wife, through the ISOs ten years ago.

When composing your ISO, work up something warm and imaginative. If you have any preexisting conditions (herpes, for instance), you may want to state that up front. Don't make yourself out to be a millionaire when you're not. The scheme inevitably backfires. The ISO column is not a forum for perjury!

<u>Cons:</u> The ISOs—like much else in life—are a crap-shoot. Some women will be wonderful and some will make you want to pretend you're someone else. Don't indulge the temptation to hide if your dream date turns out to be Brunhilde. You'd feel terrible if someone did that to you.

CLASSES: includes continuing education, night class, seminars, lectures.

<u>Pros:</u> Time and money are always in short supply but priorities are priorities and if it's a bright, curious woman you're after, take a class. Classes are not only a terrific way to meet other people, they're an opportunity to exercise your mind and talents in a way work simply doesn't offer. In a classroom environment, talking to people is as easy as finding things to talk about. If you have a rich, mellifluous voice, take a voice-over class.

James Bond fantasies? Try a class on private detective work. You're at your best when you're having fun. If you involve yourself in activities that interest you—be it ornithology or ceramics—you'll meet people (women, too!) you'll like.

<u>Cons:</u> The biggest mistake men make when trying to meet women through class factories is enrolling in copper enameling or macramé (where they're sure they'll meet women) when they'd rather take archaeology. Remember: always take the class that interests you regardless of the babe potential. When you finally meet someone, you want to have something to talk about, don't you? You'll be a lot more attract*ed* and attract*ive* to a woman with common interests. You may have to try two or three classes before you find someone who excites you but think how smart you'll be by the time you do!

AVOIDING HOOF-IN-MOUTH DISEASE

There's a tacit understanding between the sexes: men talk and women listen. We all agree to it; watch any group of people and you'll see.

But nobody wants to listen all the time. Not that amazing benefits aren't to be derived from having friends *listen to you* unbosom yourself of thoughts, feelings, and anxieties. But the advantages of LISTENING are twofold: 1) you aren't pressured to entertain, and 2) you can learn a lot about the person you're listening to.

What's so great about *active listening* is it often passes for charm. Active listeners ask "what" questions that open the door to myriad possible answers (*"What* do you like best/least about your job?" "*What's* the scariest movie you ever saw?") instead of "why" questions where there's an implied demand for justification ("*Why* did you move there?" "*Why* are women like that?"). "What" questions build rapport and building rapport is a lot more effortless than many men realize.

The hardest thing for men to do when conversing with the Fair Sex is make eye contact. But looking away, especially while she's regaling you with anecdotes about her childhood, will be construed as lack of interest. It may be a challenge, yes, but make as much eye contact as possible.

THE FIRST DATE

First dates should be a work of minimalist art. A single flower, for example, is far more eloquent than two dozen roses. Lunch dates are increasingly popular because the heavily implied eroticism of dinner dating can prove threatening to women who barely know you. Plan to meet at a museum instead or have lunch in the museum cafeteria. Grab a couple of sandwiches and eat in the park. One man I interviewed took his dates to beginner's square dancing classes. Another likes to go ice skating. Doing something physical on a first date (besides having sex!) lends itself to instant rapport. After all, most of us have the ability to laugh at our own and other people's mistakes. But if you want to develop something sexual with this woman, I do not under any circumstances advise you to initiate heavy sexual contact on the first date. First dates are for having fun and determining whether you like each other. Besides, the chances are pretty slim that you're going to successfully entreat her right off anyway. A kiss on the cheek is not only friendly, it makes her wonder why you didn't kiss her on the lips and that, my friends, will make her dwell on you *obsessively!*

WHAT NOW?

Okay, so you've had a terrific time together. You like her, she's got a great sense of humor—not to mention legs up to her eyeballs. Driving to work the next morning you find yourself smiling for no apparent reason, absently waving tense, edgy commuters into traffic ahead of you. You'd love to see her again but you don't want to appear too eager.

Now for the strategy. If she has an answering machine at home, call to reiterate what a nice time you had, thanks for coming. That's it. Do not personally leave a message with a roommate, a child, mother, or baby-sitter. Now—and this is the hard part—don't call her for three days.

It may not be pretty, but it's true: romance thrives on uncertainty. The post-date call was necessary politeness. But during your three-day hiatus, she will experience a host of emotions: excitement, disappointment . . . perhaps desire. Smart men play a little hard to get but they never play games. Don't manipulate this woman by continually disappearing for days at a time—not if you expect to have a healthy relationship.

On your second date it may be time to try something more romantic. Go to dinner. Have your palms read or get opera tickets or attend a bluegrass festival. Now is the moment to make more intimate contact (like holding hands); what this doesn't mean is cramming your tongue down her throat. Very often if a man behaves respectfully, the woman will initiate the contact. The more aggressive you are, the greater likelihood she'll balk. So act the gentleman. It's impossible for a woman to be starry-eyed with sexual desire when she's being badgered into having sex.

However much you'll want to make love, I advise you to wait. If she's the right woman, you'll have the rest of your lives to make love. Working up a healthy sexual appetite for each other is ultimately more exciting than glutting yourselves at first twinge. With that in mind, let's talk about . . .

THE FIRST MOVE

Less is more. You don't have to paw this woman to death to get your point across. Let her come to you. After reading this book you will be the master of the most sophisticated kissing techniques, but save them for the third, fourth, or even fifth date. Longer if possible. Sex quickly loses its first enchanting ardor when you fail to prolong your delights. For her, the "whole sex thing" mustn't feel rushed, compulsory, something to be gotten through. You're giving her a chance to relax, to enjoy, to experience her wonderful eroticism and your consummate skill. The truly confident have nothing to prove by getting a woman in bed in a flash!

IN CONCLUSION

So you think you've got problems finding women to date? Just be thankful you've got the option to date! Because heaven knows your mother would love to step up to the plate and make selections for you. Or there could be some kind of national service that sent you prospective mates from a pool of large, mustachioed women. Or a compulsory marriage like a draft when you're eighteen.

Regardless, I want you to put yourself in the way of meeting new people. But try to be patient. Love finds *you*, remember? You can hasten its hand but you can't force it!

7

Clothes Make the Man

Guys are goofy dressers. That's an opinion shared by most of the women I interviewed. Which is not to say that some women aren't to be found wearing lettuce-green polyester stretch slacks or plaid muumuus.

There are a million reasons to dress well—confidence, authority, sex appeal—the list goes on. We are, alas, judged by the way we are attired. Therefore the black-sock-and-sandal thing probably isn't going to project the right image for you. And having your mom, your girlfriend, or your cousin Bernie talk you into a closetful of polo shirts isn't a swift idea either.

No, you must decide for yourself, O Confused One, what kind of image you want to project, what kind of woman you want to attract, what kind of image is going to attract what kind of woman—and what feels natural and comfortable to you. And you'll have to make that image complement what you look like. The following list of common "looks" should help you get some ideas. Be forewarned that if you're fifty years old and usually wear a Rolex, the casual beach look isn't going to attract the covetous glances of young women, just raised eyebrows. Few people look more ridiculous than the middle-aged striving to appear young or the young trying to appear older.

The Julio Iglesias Look

Fitted European suit, cut in at the waist, no vent, solid color. Thin tie.

The Robert Redford Look

Textured sport jackets, turtlenecks, khaki, nubby fabrics, stressed leather jackets, loafers, cableknit sweaters.

The Don Johnson Look

Sharp, trendy, high-contrast clothing like the T-shirts under linen jackets that were popular for a while. Bomber jackets, tweed pants and white shirts, any clothing you'd see at a nightclub.

The Patrick Swayze Look

Longer hair, muscle shirts, baggy pants/shorts, tank tops, tennis shoes or thongs, a tan.

The Clint Black Look

Tight jeans, black T-shirt, cowboy hat (optional), boots, belt, attitude.

Should you set out to acquire a look? Maybe, maybe not. What you must do, however, is find a retailer you feel comfortable with, a salesperson you can talk to, and set about buying a few lady-killing items you haven't consulted your mother about! Especially in casual wear. Too many men are: 1) wearing pants that are too baggy in the butt; 2) wearing sensible collared shirts; 3) wearing T-shirts with moronic sayings; 4) wearing baggy clothing in general. Baggy clothing may be trendy, but it ain't sexy.

For those of you who are bald or balding, *do not* grow the sides out and comb them over the top of your head. It looks awful. Moreover, you're not fooling anybody. Few women express any dismay at the thought of dating bald men. I myself find certain bald men very attractive. Sean Connery is a classic example of someone whose looks *improved* once he'd lost his hair! So don't let thinning hair hold you back. Above all, don't buy an inexpensive toupee.

You owe it to yourself to get in shape and stay in shape and women find fit men just as attractive as men find fit women. Weight training has awesome effects on men's bodies so get your keister into the gym and pump some iron! Besides, what better way to meet super-attractive women?

Aftershave is nice, as is men's cologne, but don't shop price. And don't *bathe* in the stuff. Spend a little extra, use it subtly, and smell the better for it. The same goes for jewelry. Pinkie rings and multiple gold chains are out of the question!

If you have facial hair (beard and/or mustache), keep it combed and trimmed at all times. Clean-shaven? Make sure you stay that way! Few things feel worse on a woman's skin than your prickly five o'clock shadow! And don't forget to trim your nails. Have I forgotten anything?

Well, now you're ready to stand the world on its ear. You're lookin' sharp, feeling confident, and exuding animal magnetism. Most important, you're in possession of the most sublime and exquisite sexual techniques known to womankind, because you're an expert on how to DRIVE A WOMAN WILD IN BED. So it's time to go out and find yourself a beautiful, intelligent, and spirited woman upon whom to ply the fundamentals.

You've got it all!

8

The Kiss

Remember high school? We kissed as though our lives depended on it: extra drool and lots of tongue. WILD tongue. In every orifice we could get to. And that's great for high school but we're adults now and damn it, we're going to kiss like adults, aren't we?

Kissing is the first form of foreplay. Even by itself, it can be wildly exciting, terrifically sexy. But kissing, I'm afraid, is fast becoming a lost art.

Let's start with the lips. *Don't* use your tongue right off the bat. Kiss just her lips awhile. Leisurely. You might want to gently cradle her face between your hands. Nibble her lower lip. Nibble her upper lip. Keeping your tongue slightly pointed, play little fencing games with her tongue. Think "tease." As to tongue sucking—some women like it, most women don't.

Explore her gum line a little. Her upper palate. Her teeth. All are sensitive. Vary tongue kisses with lip kisses. Kisses can be a fine main course; sometimes they are just part of what's on the menu.

We used to administer "wet-willies" in high school, too, remember? That was when you inserted your tongue into her ear in some weird kind of simulated intercourse. Wet-willies, while not always . . . er, taste-ful? . . . are fun. The trick is, you don't cram your tongue in her ear, just delicately probe its folds. Breathe. It'll give her shivers and make her giggle.

The nape of her neck (just below the hairline in the back) is very erogenous. Your breath alone will make her quiver. Do quick little running kisses over the back of her hand, up her arm, across her back and down her spine. There are tender downy hairs in the small of her back, all of which you should tickle with your breath.

Gently bite a buttock. The backs of her knees need nibbling and so do her toes (if they're fresh from the bathtub!). Take a toe in your mouth and slide it in and out. Vary your kisses (one on her thigh, her stomach, her shoulder). Then you can ascend to the control panel: her breasts.

The size of a woman's breasts has nothing to do with their sensitivity. A lot of men think bigger breasts are less sensitive and smaller breasts are more sensitive. Not true. Breasts have varying sensitivity, especially at differ-ent times of the month.

First of all, gently push her breasts together. This makes it easier to switch from one to the other and back again.

Now, with your tongue extended and your lips pulled away from her skin, lick around her nipple. It's impor-tant that your lips not touch her actual flesh right now, that air be able to circulate. Why? It feels better. The sensation isn't "smothered." Nipple sucking is nice, too, but be sure to start out with just your tongue so her nip-ples can peak. Peaked nipples are at their maximum sensitivity.

Many women like having their nipples *very lightly* nib-bled. If you use your finger to stimulate them, make sure it's very wet and run it around the peak of her nipple like you would a wine glass. Blowing on a wet nipple feels wonderful!

Try different methods of seduction like caressing her with various textures—a rough cotton bath towel, a piece of satin, a feather dipped in scented oil. Be playful. Blindfold her and make her guess what you're using. Are you into honey, chocolate, syrup, grapes, or whipped cream? See just how much fun produce can be!

These are the erogenous zones you should commit to memory:

- the lips
- the tongue
- the teeth
- the palate
- the gums
- the orbital bone (eyebrows)
- the temple
- the ears
- the earlobes
- the nape of her neck
- the spine
- the buttocks
- the backs of her knees
- the toes
- the soles of her feet
- the insides of her thighs
- the lower abdomen
- the nipples
- the palms of her hands

As you're nibbling earlobes and ravishing nipples, remember to savor the heady perfume of her flesh!

9

Bodytalk

THE HOWS OF BODYTALK

Rule number one: When you're dealing with a woman on the subject of sex, never ask her a direct question. Example:

> You: "Was it good for you?"
>
> Her: "Uh, yeah. Sure it was, honey."

Many women have a kind of crablike privacy when it comes to sex. Pry off the shell and you kill the crab. When you're trying to sound a woman out about something, it pays to be indirect. Indirectness has traditionally been the woman's way. Women, since time immemorial, have used it with devastating effectiveness on the men in their lives. That's why your partner always seems to know more about you than you know about her. I call this technique the "Third Person Invisible" because you'll always be making reference to someone or something that isn't in the room. Example:

You: (casually) "Gee, honey, I read today that
         75 percent of all couples experiment with
         anal intercourse. Do you think that's
         true?"

Her: "You did? Where?"

You: "At the office. Somebody left a *Cosmo* lying
         around."

Her: "Does that sort of thing interest you?"

You: "Gosh, I don't know. I never thought
         about it before. But before I'd even
         consider it, I'd have to know how you felt
         about it."

Her: "Well, I don't think it's immoral or
         anything."

You: "Oh, it's not immoral, I don't think. The
         couples interviewed said they really
         enjoyed it."

Okay. Is she going to drop on all fours and rip her
clothes off? No, probably not. But you have started an
interesting conversation, haven't you? She'll start to
wonder if this isn't something you have a secret hankering for. Her awareness of the entire subject will be
heightened. Maybe she'll even start leafing through
back issues of *Cosmopolitan* trying to find that mysterious
article. Then, when the issue is brought up in bed, it
won't be such a bolt out of the blue. Of course, none of
this coyness is necessary with a woman who can openly
discuss her sexuality. There are many, many women who
can say "penis" without blushing. But many can't.

In addition to various "articles," use fictitious "acquaintances," too. Example:

> You: "You know, I was talking to Bob today and he said his wife liked being spanked. Can you believe it?"
>
> Her: "Spanked? You've got to be kidding."
>
> You: "No, really. He gave her a little swat on the behind one day and she begged him for more."
>
> Her: "My God! Who are these people? I think that's depraved!"

It doesn't take a junior Freud to figure out that spanking games aren't this woman's cup of tea. Save it for your fantasies.

The Kama Sutra

The Kama Sutra is a famous (or infamous!) collection of sexually explicit illustrations by an Indian named Vatsyayana from around the first century A.D. They've been printed and reprinted so many times it would be nearly impossible for you not to unearth them in your local bookstore. The Kama Sutra (and like illustrations) can be very useful in starting a sexual dialogue. Example:

> You're canoodling on the couch together, perusing the wild book "Bob" just gave you. You come across an illustration of a woman fellating her partner. "Gee, look at that," you say. "I'm getting a chubby just thinking about it. What have you seen that makes you wild?"

You've neatly accomplished two objectives here: you've stated very nicely that oral sex is a priority and you've opened the door for her to discuss her preferences as well. The object is to speak generally about sex, not personally, when you're divining a woman's wishes. Try to be as natural as possible!

THE WHERES OF BODYTALK

Cars

Where is almost as important as how. Certain places are more conducive to sharing sexual intimacies. The car, for example. You're in a physically and psychologically confining space, but not forced to make eye contact, nor "facing off." I consider this to be one of the best places for discussing sex or anything requiring tact and diplomacy.

Food

Sex has long been predicated on shared food rituals, so dinner is my next choice. While you are facing each other discussing sex, you can also occupy yourselves with the business of eating. Food is inherently sexual.

Phones

You can't read her face over the phone, but the heightened anonymity of discussing sex on the phone often makes it easier to be honest. After you've known her awhile, you can tell her all the deliciously naughty things you want to do to her.

Bed

Bed is the last place you should have prolonged conversations, sexual or otherwise—especially the airing of petty grievances. Why? Some places must be sacred. Safe spaces. You are never more naked or more vulnerable than when you're sleeping or making love. Bed becomes a sort of harbor, a special sanctuary to retreat to. In fact, all financial, sexual, religious, or political discussions ought to be directed elsewhere. Feelings, good or bad, are often rooted strongly to a place, just as memories are to music. Let your bed be a vacation from conflict.

Keep your eyes—and your ears—open for any inoffensive way to jump-start a sexual dialogue. Communication is the key to almost everything.

10

Condom Etiquette

There are so many reasons to wear a condom.

The fatal HIV virus (which leads to AIDS) is only one of a funhouse of exciting diseases you can contract if you don't. Herpes is painful and incurable, though treatable, and humiliating. Chlamydia will make a woman sterile. Gonorrhea is highly infectious and untreated syphilis can make you insane or sterile or kill you.

What's so sad is that it took all this to rethink monogamy.

The bottom line is men need to wear condoms. There's more at stake here than the diminished sensitivity of your penis.

If you ask a person with the HIV virus how he contracted the disease, he might say, "Because I was afraid I'd embarrass my partner if I whipped out a condom." You then might think to yourself, "This wonderful person is dying of a terminal illness. All because he didn't want to embarrass himself or his lover?" And, of course, it would seem tragic and ridiculous. And completely avoidable.

We all want to be liked and loved. How many of us are

willing to run the risk of losing someone's regard by asking him/her to fortify against any diseases they might carry? Especially when most of us have an unshakable belief that "other people" get AIDS? It's easier just to sweep the whole thing aside, dismissing our recklessness as the daring of passion.

Meanwhile, the disease is spreading and multiplying and mutating . . .

The most awkward thing we find about using a condom isn't putting it on—it's gracefully introducing the damn thing in the first place. The solution is, like many things, both obvious and simple. Ordinarily neither partner, for instance, feels uncomfortable when a woman halts sexual proceedings to insert a diaphragm. Well, condoms are contraceptives, too. It stands to follow that neither you nor your partner will feel uncomfortable if you just grab a condom off the nightstand. You don't need to say anything. No explanations, justifications, or rationalizations are necessary. The trick is wherever you are, have the condom within arm's reach. Take it out and slip it on. Condoms aren't a big deal unless you make them one. They're like discussions with your kids about sex: if you feel uncomfortable, you're going to communicate your discomfort to your children.

Where we go wrong, of course, is having sex (the most intimate of communications) with people we don't even know well enough to discuss transmittable disease. There's something hugely bizarre and twisted about that. However, you'll have to introduce the subject at some point; condoms can't be worn forever. If a relationship looks as though it's going somewhere, most people tactfully sound each other out about "questionable" liaisons they may have had in the past. This is about as scientific as consulting a Ouija board. There

are no "questionable" liaisons anymore because everyone is a candidate for disease. If no "problem" is found,
most couples proceed (unwisely) to engage in unpro-
tected intercourse.

Many people think the solution is having a blood test.
If you want to initiate a conversation about blood (or
urine analyses for some diseases other than AIDS),
under no circumstances make it sound like she's the
one who's suspect. Try something approximating:

> "You know, I'm getting pretty tired of condoms. I
> want to feel you, to really feel you. But I don't want
> to pass anything on if I've got something so I'm
> going to get a blood test. And look, I'd feel a whole
> lot more comfortable if we both knew we were
> healthy. You can't fool around anymore. If you
> come down and get a blood test with me, we'll both
> be sure."

Realize, however, that even with a blood screen you
could have been contaminated with the HIV virus in the
last six months but not have it show up on your test.
This is known as "the window period," and to be safe
you should continue using condoms until the six
months pass and you get another test.

Female condoms are another option, although, as of
this writing, they are largely unavailable in the United
States. They are a rubber pouchlike device with a ring
on either end. The woman inserts the first ring deep
into her vagina, near the cervix. The second ring hangs
outside the vagina. Until more is known about their effi-
cacy, I advise you to stick with the condom for men—it's
far easier to sheathe the pestle than the mortar!

11

Overheard

Most women are very diplomatic. It's an exercise in subtlety just to understand them. But now's your chance to get in on their real preferences and opinions. To understand once and for all their feelings about men and their illustrious members! A hand-picked selection:

"The sexiest thing about a man is his hands. Nobody believes me when I say that. A friend asked me once if I would ignore some gorgeous man with an ass like an ice skater just because the guy sitting next to me had nice hands. Of course not. But men's hands continue to hold me spellbound. I especially like strong weathered hands with calluses and big knuckles. Oddly enough, they look so gentle."

Vivien, 34, stockbroker

"Men have this really annoying habit of calling and not immediately introducing themselves. They either assume you know who they are from the first hello, or that no other men call you, or that you've been so consumed, waiting for their call, you knew right away. I resent it. Some guys even play this guessing game with you—'Who do you think this is?'—as though by giving them more than three possible suspects you're an automatic slut. It's so territorial. Now I just hang up."

Belinda, 21, student

"I met my husband in a nightclub. Believe me, I wasn't dressed like Mother Teresa. Now that we're married he doesn't want me wearing makeup or heels let alone a sexy miniskirt. It drives me crazy. Seeing as how I'm his property now, I'm supposed to neuter myself so I won't be attractive to other men. His excuse is, 'I don't want other guys thinking you're available.' Yeah. Meanwhile, he leers at every girl wearing what he won't let me wear. What a double standard! I wish he'd grow up and realize that just because I like feeling attractive doesn't mean I want to 'cruise for guys.' I just want to be glad I'm a woman."

Julia, 26, administrative assistant

"I can't resist a sense of humor. Most men think that means they have to be a comedian twenty-four hours a day. It doesn't. It means having a humorous outlook on life. Maybe it means the ability to put things in their proper perspective. Some men are just so type-A about everything. No wonder they're all dropping dead of heart attacks."

Francesca, vice president, advertising

"My boyfriend takes a fiendish glee in telling me how beautiful he finds this or that actress, my friends, anyone. Why? Why is it necessary I know who the hell he finds attractive? Sometimes I think he plays this game with me so I won't think I'm pretty and won't leave him. I might leave him all right, but it won't be because I suddenly got this attitude about how great I am. I'll leave him because he's an inconsiderate jerk."

Lisa, 27, teacher

"It's that 'male bonding' thing I can't get over. Oh, I think it's important they have that and everything, it's just I don't fully understand it. Why don't they ever really talk? It seems like all they do—openly or subtly—is compete with each other. What I find especially amusing is when my fiancé gets a phone call from one of his buddies. He'll be talking to me one way, then he gets on the phone and sounds totally different. 'Manlier.' It's too funny. I'd like to tape him sometime. He always pretends not to know what I'm talking about when I point this out."

Yolanda, 32, sales rep

"Penises are much sweeter than men want us to acknowledge. Even when they're erect, they look so cute—as though they need protection. Of course men like to think their penises are weapons of pillage and destruction. I'm sure they wouldn't like it if they knew women felt *maternal* toward them!"

Gladys, 62, real estate agent

"Men are so afraid of looking as though they don't know everything—directions, tools, the 'right' way to do things . . . you name it. I wish they'd relax and

be human. Maybe even let their partner be 'right'
for a change. They probably wouldn't mind doing
that if we were stranded on a deserted island somewhere but if everyone else found out, they'd crawl
under a rock and die."

Sally, 31, comedian

12

(Don't) Do It!

Ah, yes. The gaffe, the blunder, the galling faux pas. The look in her eyes when your offhand remark is misconstrued or when your ex-wife's underwear is found wedged beneath the mattress. Men walk on eggshells to avoid saying the wrong thing to women, then wind up saying it anyway. "I try to be sensitive!" they wail. "What do they want from us?"

Good manners start with cultivating good taste. That means filing the matched set of Playmate mugs and your porno collection. Save that anecdote about losing the handcuff key at the Motel 6 in Laredo for when you're better acquainted. I'm not asking that you magically transform yourself overnight; it's hard for any of us to change. Just be more aware of what you say and what you do and how that affects her perceptions of you.

1. **Get rid of the ceiling mirrors, bearskin rugs, and posters of naked women.**

   The less overpowering your bedroom is, the more comfortable she'll feel being in it.

2. **Remove all vestiges of former female occupancy.**

That means underwear, cold cream, long hair in the
hair brush, extra toothbrushes, mateless earrings,
barrettes, and lingering perfume on your pillowcase. No woman appreciates feeling as though she's
one of many.

3. **Don't automatically assume she knows who you are
when you call.**

Announce your full name the first several calls and
your first name thereafter. For reasons known only
to themselves, men play games on the phone, possibly to determine how many other men call her.

4. **Don't refer to or qualify women by their hair color.**

No one likes being reduced to a hair color, a skin
color, etc. Any conversation that begins, "I saw this
blonde, okay?" is bound to deteriorate into a squab-
ble.

5. **Don't assume you can freely utter racial slurs in
front of a woman.**

If knowing that bigotry is ignorant and hurtful isn't
enough, realize that a lot of women are highly sensi-
tized to these issues. Helena, a twenty-six-year-old
loan processor, put it this way: "If he thinks these
things about African, Latin, and Asian Americans,
what does he really think about women?"

6. **If a woman rejects your advances, do not accuse her
of being a lesbian.**

If you, personally, are not guilty of such behavior,
pat yourself on the back because these kinds of

knee-jerk retaliatory statements aren't rare. Sometimes women don't gracefully discourage a man's attentions—in part because they're scared. Having a
bigger, stronger person come onto you is always a
little intimidating. Whatever she said or did, there's
no excuse for speculation about her sexual predilec-
tion.

7. **Save the bathroom humor for your men friends.**

Most women don't like the Three Stooges for the
same reasons they dislike fart jokes and the other
supposedly humorous scatological oddities men
enjoy. Women largely perceive men who dwell on
bathroom humor as childish.

8. **Don't volunteer information about your past relationships.**

Telling a date that your ex was a model or an exotic
dancer puts impossible pressure on the woman to
compete. She'll be suspicious about your present
feelings for your ex. If you run into a former flame
while on a date, no matter what your feelings may
be, don't pause to chat. Say hello and move on—unless, of course, you want your date's handbag buried
in your skull.

9. **Even if you've paid for dinner, or several dinners,
and your date returns to your apartment with you,
don't automatically assume she plans to sleep with
you.**

Even if she dresses sexy, acts sexy, kisses you and
professes a ravening sexual interest in you, if at
some point she says no, *don't force her to have sex.* All

women reserve the right to do with their bodies what they want—not what *you* want. Ownership papers are not signed over after a couple of drinks.

10. Never display sexual interest in her friends or sisters.

This is the most heinous crime you can commit against a woman. Even if her sister is the most seductive, drop-dead gorgeous woman you've ever met, forget it. Unless a relationship is in its most preliminary stages, sisters and friends are strictly off limits. The easiest way to understand this is to imagine your wife or girlfriend in bed with one of *your* pals or *your* brother. Does that bring it home for you?

13

Turning Her On

We've all heard about aphrodisiacs. Spanish flies that make you want to hump the stick shift. Pulverized rhinoceros horn that makes a stallion out of a land turtle. Fun stuff—but fairy tales. To get into a woman's bed, first you have to get into a woman's head.

This is a chapter on foreplay before foreplay. Research indicates that women who are orgasmic are women who *think* a lot of sexy stuff before they have sex. How can you get your partner to think sexy thoughts? Read on, read on . . .

A woman I'll call Brenda said her bedroom sessions were pretty humdrum until she read that women need a lot more mental foreplay than men do. Stimulating a woman's sexual imagination is just as important as stimulating anything else. Just trying to stimulate her body isn't going to do it. That's what a woman would do if she were trying to stimulate a man. You will have to be a lot more inventive than that. But it's so easy—in many ways easier—than the traditional "put thumb here" methods that have gotten you nowhere in the past. What Brenda did, for instance, was embark on an erotic adventure in her mind the minute she hit the car after work. So by the time she was home, she was foaming at the mouth and ready to go. Even then, she reports, it didn't begin to compare to the thrill she got when her husband sent her naughty notes or indecent proposals.

STRATEGIES

The first thing you need to do to set the stage for wonderful sex is get rid of the kids. Once a month (at least) you should farm them out to doting grandparents so you and the missus can get to know each other again. Don't expect to have terrific sex all the time after children are born. Then it becomes even more of a challenge for a woman to switch gears—something a lot of men have trouble understanding. Spontaneity goes right out the window.

The next plan you might want to map out is the one thing you can do that's different—a change of locale, for instance. Most of us have sex on the bed. Why not opt for the kitchen floor instead? Or the living room couch? Or any one of the "101 Best Places for a Quickie" (Chapter 23) listed this book? It's a lot easier to "rediscover" each other in an exotic locale, even if that means the back seat of your car.

Even if the bedroom is the only place orthopedically you want to make love, you can still put satin sheets on the bed, install a ceiling mirror, or light a dozen candles. Get a lava lamp and play "Free Bird" (if you have a sense of humor)—anything that's fun and imaginative. Imagination is half of lovemaking. And any woman will tell you that imaginative lovers are in *very* short supply!

Woo Me, Win Me, Make Me a Woman

Ah, the sheer, unadulterated, gut-wrenching, heart-rending, hair-ripping, nail-clenching power of the written word! Words are the biggest seducer of all. That's why I want you to get off your high horse of machismo and find a poem that perfectly expresses your feelings! If you can write her a poem, so much the better. Goddesses love custom tributes to their divinity! A poem is the first step you're going to take to heighten her sexual sensitivies. You will leave the poem, neatly printed (not typed or hacked out on the computer!), on any of the following:

- her pillow
- the refrigerator
- the bathroom mirror
- her purse
- the steering wheel of her car
- in a letter
- accompanied by flowers
- accompanied by lingerie
- attached to the dog's collar
- in a Single's Ad addressed specifically to her (yes, you'll have to point it out to her)
- taped over the TV screen
- taped to her desk at work
- next to her panties in the underwear drawer
- framed by her bed
- on the lid of the washing machine (unless it's your turn to do the laundry this week)
- via singing telegram
- or, recite the poem, tape yourself, and put the cassette in her car

Erotic literature can be terrifically sexy when it's whispered over a pillow or on a candlelit couch. Most women aren't offended by sexually explicit material—try reading a romance novel sometime, or watching daytime TV. It'll blow your socks off. The difference between male- versus female-oriented erotica is not its sexual content but its feeling content. Male erotica, not unlike locker-room conversation, is full of the anatomical and the acrobatic. Sexually predatory stuff. Female erotica is all about ecstasy and dizzying surrenders and the rapture of consummated love. Compare this with *Penthouse* Letters to the Editor: I happened across a story about an amputee and her boyfriend who liked to have sex with her stump; a dominatrix and her clients; finally, a woman who blew her nose on her lover's penis and used it as a lubricant. Can you see the difference?

The adult film industry is even catching on. Now you have a choice in what movies you'd like to watch—male-oriented or female-oriented. So far as I can see, though, the differences are minimal but the trend itself is important. We're beginning (after thousands of years) to finally consider the differences between how men and women become sexually aroused.

Carriage Rides

Or hay rides. Depends where you live, right? What a wonderful romantic way to get things going. One man I interviewed proposed to a woman in a horse-drawn carriage. He presented her with a small bouquet of roses, their stems circled by an engagement ring.

Or how about that old standby, flowers? And if you want to spice up giving flowers a little, send something else I call:

The Package

A woman I interviewed (whom I'll call Amanda) was at work one day, bored, a little moody because her lover was away on business. After lunch she received a mysterious delivery from him and when she opened it, she found a gorgeous garter-and-panty set, a satin blindfold, and a note. The note instructed her to go home immediately after work, eat, wash, put on the lingerie and the blindfold, and lie down on the bed. She was to be finished and waiting by 8:00. At 8:01, her lover let himself into the apartment, quietly disrobed in the foyer, and—never speaking above a whisper and *never* letting her remove the blindfold—made wild passionate jungle love to her. Amanda gets emotional every time she talks about it. Her words? "My God, I hope he never leaves. How will I ever find anyone who knows how to do those kinds of things?"

The Freeway of Love (Or: the Note, the Candle, the Snack, the Rose Petals, the Bath, and the Bed)

When Angela came home one day, she found a note tacked on the door that read: "When you enter the Nile, you become my Cleopatra." Smiling, she pulled the note off the door and walked inside—only to find yet another note. This one said: "Take this candle, fair damsel, light it with yon matchstick, and discover the secret treasure buried in the refrigerator." When Angela opened the refrigerator, she found chilled champagne and something that passed for caviar awaiting her consumption. From the door to the candle to the refrigerator was a trail of rose petals (you can also use Hershey's

Kisses or Christmas ribbon) and there were more rose petals going up the stairs where another note awaited: "I languish, my lady." The petals led into the bathroom where her lover was neck-high in bubbles, more candles were shedding a soft glow, and "Unforgettable" was playing on the boom box. He winked. She undressed. They ate, wallowing in bubbly indolence until he carried her to the bed where a single rose lay on a satin pillowcase.

Angela will never stop talking about it.

The Lunch Wagon

Francine was at work one humdrum day. Right about 9:30, a messenger came in with a package for her. When she unwrapped it, she found a pink satin teddy, a bottle of perfume, and a note. The note, anonymous but in a strangely familiar handwriting ("what *is* he doing?") told her to go to a particular hotel at 12:15 wearing nothing but the teddy, her heels, and an overcoat. Francine smiled and shook her head but there was an unmistakable gleam in her eye.

In the hotel room, there he was—Dan, her boyfriend, buck naked with a Christmas ribbon wrapped around his. . . . Anyway, they shared some laughs and a glass of champagne and he devoured her for half an hour on the bed. "Going downstairs was the hardest part," Francine told me later. "I was so self-conscious. I just knew everyone was looking, knowing there was only one thing we could have been doing for an hour in a hotel room."

Francine is one of the few women I know who talks about her steady boyfriend like he was a Lover.

The Abduction

Every woman has a fantasy where she's swept off her feet. Steve knew this, so when he got a little money together, he met his girlfriend after work one Friday afternoon in the back of a huge stretch limo that pulled right up to her office door. Steve was wearing a black tux jacket, jeans, a splash of cologne, and carried not only a dozen roses but a book of love poems. When Trish, his girlfriend, came downstairs, she nearly screamed with delight.

The limo took them to the airport. Steve, cleverly, had their packed bags in the trunk. They petted like teenagers in the limo, cast lovesick glances at each other on the plane, and spent the entire weekend doing the wild thing at a bed-and-breakfast in upstate New York. Trish swears she gets wet just remembering that incredible weekend with Steve.

Eating In, Eating Out

As Mark liked to say, "One kid is a family—*three* kids are a herd," so when he saw Suzanne getting frazzled with cooking and working and being a mom, he dispatched the children to grandparents for the weekend. Mark knew he couldn't even boil water so he hired a friend who was a chef at a Northern Italian restaurant to come in Saturday night to whip something up in his kitchen. In the living room, Mark put a red-and-white-checked tablecloth on the coffee table (less formal than the dining room), a dripping candle in the neck of a wine bottle, and Italian opera on the stereo. When Suzanne came home she was served a scrumptious meal in her own home by a "weird guy in a chef's hat, but boy, could he cook!" Mark was very romantic and attentive. After dinner, they danced to Mark's collection of big band tunes, and he swept her off her feet and into a bubble bath where they made soapy love before moving to the bedroom. "It was one of the best nights of my life," Suzanne said. "I know I'm the luckiest woman in the world."

PAY ATTENTION!

These are only a few of a billion ideas for heightening your lover's sexual sensitivities before foreplay. Every one of these women reported being very sexually excited before they had sex, but you don't have to go to such extremes to get the same results. One of the first things an unforgettable lover must learn is how to keep the romance alive in his relationship on a day-to-day basis. That means being affectionate and attentive most of the time. Not *all* of the time, but more than you're probably used to. This doesn't come naturally to most men. It is interesting to note, however, that 100 percent of the women I interviewed who were cheating on their husbands or lovers reported feeling "neglected" in their relationship. They didn't stray because some hunk had a larger penis or more money. They strayed because NOT ENOUGH ATTENTION WAS PAID TO THEM.

Goddesses become very surly when ignored. The problem is, most men express their affection by their actions: "Well, I'm here, aren't I?" "What are you griping about? It's not like I cheat on you or beat you or anything!" "I provide for this family very well, thank you!" But guess what? For 99.99 percent of the women out there, you may be tending to their practical needs but not their romantic ones. Women need lots of nonsexual affection (this means affection that is not always a prelude to sex) and "I love yous" and maybe an occasional bouquet or some other token of your esteem. Try doing something special once a month especially if you're training to become legendary as opposed to luckless.

14

The Oral Report and Dr. G-spot

Oral sex. For some women, it's the only way they're going to have an orgasm. For your edification, this does not mean they are lesbians. If you're from the school that holds that not all women have a glorious odor, instead of hurting her feelings, suggest you take a bath together. Baths cleanse the area a lot better than showers.

Most men are eager to administer their oral talents. Unfortunately, most women can't explain exactly what it is they want. The first thing you're going to do is memorize what is and is not especially sensitive about the female genitalia:

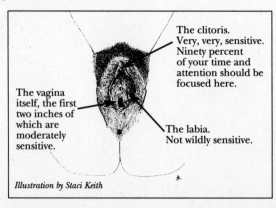

The clitoris. Very, very, sensitive. Ninety percent of your time and attention should be focused here.

The vagina itself, the first two inches of which are moderately sensitive.

The labia. Not wildly sensitive.

Illustration by Staci Keith

The clitoris (as I'm sure you know) is the most important part of a woman's sexual anatomy. It's like the entire head of your penis shrunk down to an area smaller than a pea. The clitoris is so sensitive, it requires a "hood"—hence, the clitoral hood, which serves to protect it. This, too, is highly sensitive. The friction from this sheath of skin is what precipitates most female orgasms. (Some women experience vaginal orgasms, too.)

THE FOLLOWING METHOD IS THE BEST, EASIEST, AND MOST EFFECTIVE WAY TO BRING YOUR PARTNER TO ORGASM. Even women who report having orgasms without this particular method say the orgasm is far more intense and quicker to achieve this way.

AGENDA

1. Lie directly between her legs.
2. Spread her vaginal lips far apart.
3. Locate her clitoris.
4. With just your tongue, slightly pointed *(keeping your lips away from her vagina),* flick lightly across her clitoris. Side to side.
5. (Optional) Insert a finger into the vagina itself, twisting it in and out.

The trick is to keep your mouth off the clitoris and to lick lightly. You can't "smother" the clitoris with your lips or you'll deaden the sensation. Most men make the mistake of licking too hard. You will tire at first. Should this occur, try lying not between her legs but off to one side at a perpendicular angle. This means your tongue flicking up and down will feel side to side to her. Or, if you're directly between her legs, shake your head, not just your tongue. Remember to keep the pressure light and your tongue slightly pointed. Do note that one side of her clitoris is more sensitive than the other. If she doesn't know which, experiment. That's the side you want to lie on so she can get your down stroke.

It's that simple!

A lot of men ask, "How long should I do it?" and I answer, "How long can you last?" This is where stamina becomes important. At first, you'll have to build up to it. The strain of keeping your lips back is what challenges your enthusiasm. Go for four minutes your first night and tack on another minute every week. But trust me, it's your prowess with your tongue (not your penis) that will make a legendary lover out of you!

One gentleman approached me with an enterprising (and amusing) idea. When he's tired, he plugs in this large, flat-headed vibrator he bought, sticks his tongue on his lover's clitoris, and applies the vibrator to his chin, the vibration from which (I assume) drives his partner into orgasmic ecstasy. How's that for determination!

THE G-SPOT

The fabled G-spot is not easy to locate. Women have a hard time finding it, too. And not all women believe they have one. The method, however, is simple: with her lying on her back, insert one or two fingers all the way into her vagina with your palm facing up. Now bend them slightly. The inside of a woman's vagina feels like a ribbed condom but between her bladder and her pelvis exists an area that is very sensitive. You may or may not be able to distinguish its shape (which is roundish), so let her directions be your guide. Once you've located it, she might initially feel the urge to—of all things—urinate. Yes! Nature is a scream. But don't worry, she probably won't urinate on you. This feeling passes and then the sensation becomes pleasurable. Or it may never become pleasurable. It's one of those things. But don't keep rubbing if she says she doesn't like it. And never rub too hard. You don't have anything to prove to her or to yourself.

Even if your partner enjoys this as a form of foreplay, she may or may not be able to climax from G-spot stimulation alone. But what the G-spot is for everybody is fun to find. It's a humorous sexual adventure and heaven knows we need to laugh more in bed.

The G-spot (for those of you who asked) was named after the man who "discovered" it, Dr. Grafenberg. What makes this guy think he was the first to find it baffles me and he has some nerve naming it after himself. If I were you, I'd give it your own name. That way you can be sure it'll come when you call . . . !

15

The Heart of the Matter

Nothing—not oral sex, not "hand jobs"—feels as *satisfying* as intercourse. Even women who never have orgasms during intercourse say the same thing: it's a very sexy, emotionally satisfying experience.

Stores that sell sexual paraphernalia are stacked to the rafters with books detailing a thousand bizarre positions. These books usually include photographs of a couple, the woman's legs lifted at a 90 degree angle (position one), a 60 degree angle (position two), a 30 degree angle (position three) . . . I think you get the picture. No, I'm not going to detail sexual acrobatics in this chapter. Instead, I shall cover all the basic positions with suggestions on how to make them more enjoyable for both you and your partner.

MISSIONARY

As one story goes, two missionaries in the South Sea islands were making love on the beach. They copulated face-to-face. The natives, seeing them, found this wildly amusing because the natives themselves only mated doggie-style. How the name "missionary style" managed to circulate off the island, I have no idea, but I'm sure the missionaries were mortified.

The missionary position is when two people are making love face-to-face, the woman lying on her back with the man on top. It is also a church-sanctioned position, which has given it an unwarranted reputation for dullness. To spice things up, however, a (flexible) woman can put her ankles on her partner's shoulders (thus affording maximum penetration) or spread her legs as far apart as possible.

Improving the position

The problem for women during missionary-style intercourse is the lack of stimulation to the clitoris. *Most women need clitoral stimulation in order to climax.* I say most because there are women who say they aren't sure their clitorises are being stimulated when they climax. I personally believe (and research corroborates) that when a woman climaxes, the clitoris is being at least indirectly stimulated. Touching your partner's clitoris may be like doing a one-arm push-up at first, but you'll quickly get the knack of it. The trick is to put your thumb (your wet thumb) above or beside her clitoris, not directly on it. You don't need to move it at all. The movement of your body will do the work for you. You can try "riding high in the saddle" so that your penis or your pelvic bone comes into contact with her clitoris, but how good can it feel to bend your penis in half? That's why I recommend you stimulate her manually or allow her to assist herself. A lot of men have a problem with their partner masturbating during intercourse ("By God, if anyone's having an orgasm around here, I'm going to be responsible for it"), which is unfortunate because it can free them up to enjoy other things—their partner's breasts, for instance. Self-assistance is a good idea some of the time. What's great is you can watch (very exciting) and learn the way she touches herself. The next time, you can do it yourself.

WOMAN ON TOP

All your favorite things and you've got a front-row seat! As the name implies, the man is lying on his back and the woman's on top controlling the rhythm, penetration, and, generally, the whole show. She can pivot around and face your feet if she chooses, or she can balance her weight on the balls of her feet. If she's extremely flexible, she can do a split over your penis.

Improving the position

You can improve this position the same way you can improve missionary-style intercourse: by stimulating her clitoris. In this position, it's a cinch to locate. Many women find it easier to climax on top, so here's an opportunity to maximize. A note here on stimulating a woman's clitoris with your finger: most men rub too hard. The important thing is to keep your finger well lubricated, use an extremely light pressure (unless otherwise directed), and move your finger side to side. This is not a scratch-card we're dealing with here, it's a clitoris, so exercise some delicacy!

And don't forget to tell her how great she looks.

DOGGIE-STYLE

Comedian Dennis Miller once quipped about doggie-style intercourse, "You really know you're at the helm of the bobsled!"

Doggie-style (intercourse with the woman on all fours with her partner penetrating her from behind) possesses a wonderful kind of animal excitement. Eons ago, the human vagina slanted backward, not forward, so perhaps making love from behind rekindles atavistic impulses.

The women I interviewed had plenty to say about doggie-style intercourse.

"I love doing it doggie-style," one college student claimed. "But my boyfriend never makes the most of it. He just sort of pounds away, not saying anything. I'd like it if he grabbed my behind and really got into it—you know, with enthusiasm. I enjoy the feeling of being dominated and I want him to *possess* me, to make animal noises, maybe even talk dirty. I just know it can be better than this."

Most women (I will hazard to say) like being dominated in bed. Nowhere else—just bed. But men are afraid to really let themselves grab and grunt, to let go, and that's why women are saying men have no "passion" anymore. Doggie-style affords you great opportunities to be passionate (to even talk "dirty," if she likes) and—unless she's got eyes in the back of her head—the freedom to look ridiculous doing it.

Once again, you must locate her clitoris. In this position, it's easier for the woman to do it herself. Or let her use a vibrator. A vibrator actually seems to work best. Just for the record, a woman's biggest fear during doggie-style is that you're going to accidentally penetrate her rectum. Nobody likes being surprised that way.

SPOONING

Picture two spoons nestled back-to-front in a drawer—hence the name. Also known as "Sunday morning sex" probably because it's comfortable and easygoing and a good way to hide bad breath!

The scenario: You're both on your sides with her in front of you. She parts her legs and—*voila!* In you go. You can reach across and feel her breasts or stimulate her clitoris. Or both. This is possibly the only comfortable position for pregnant women.

Improving the position

When copulating (don't you love that word?), most men thrust in and out, in and out like pistons in an engine. Nothing exciting. Far better to move slowly but forcefully. That means drawing your penis out very slowly, pausing half a second, then driving it home again hard. A lot of men forget how exciting it can be when they vary their rhythm (or the depth of their penetration). I recommend you try this with all positions, not just spooning. Sometimes it's nice to start out in a spoon, then proceed to doggie-style with your partner lying flat on her stomach.

BETWEEN HER BREASTS

I suspect there are a lot more men in this country who like fat women than will admit it. And bigger girls have bigger breasts. You can make a big girl feel incredibly womanly by using her size as an asset during sex—specifically, having sex between her breasts.

Most couples who are able to partake of these fleshly enjoyments do so with the woman on her back and the man sliding his penis between her breasts. You're not however, getting the maximum effect either visually or physically. There's always a better way of doing things.

Improving the position

You're on your back (for a change!). Your partner is between your legs with her breasts hanging over your penis. With lubricant, press her breasts around your penis while she rocks back and forth. This way you get maximum cleavage, and such a view! Let her know she's the wildest, sexiest woman you know and give her a good tongue-lashing afterward.

69

Somehow 69 is one of those positions that is always more exquisitely choreographed in our imagination than is ever gracefully executed in real life. Sixty-nine is when you perform cunnilingus on your partner while she's fellating your penis. It's terrifically exciting—all those sights and smells. It's better than a Grand Canyon tour. But it's challenging to concentrate on administering your oral talents on her when your own orgasm is seconds away.

Improving the position

Most couples attempt 69 with the man on top and the woman beneath. This isn't optimal because fellatio requires some head and neck mobility and a mattress is too stiff a plane of resistance. Far better for her to be on top or for her to lean her head over the edge of the bed. This will require you to stand or kneel—sometimes 69 is best performed in a big cushy chair. Be sure you remember to spread her vaginal lips far apart. She'll feel your tongue more keenly that way.

ANAL INTERCOURSE

In American culture, anal intercourse is treated either like a forbidden erotic adventure or something tantamount to homosexuality. It is neither. Anal intercourse is widely practiced in countries where a woman's hymen must be intact until marriage or as a preventative against pregnancy. It is, however, like all intercourse, a high-risk activity—that is, the likelihood of the transmission of the HIV virus is very high unless both of you are HIV negative or you wear a condom. And use a *new* condom if you switch from anal to vaginal sex.

Improving the position

Many couples experiment with anal intercourse at some point in their relationship. They usually make three mistakes: 1) the woman doesn't realize that anal sex, like coffee and cigarettes, is an acquired taste; 2) the man, intending to be gentle, usually ends up hurting her more; 3) they don't use an over-the-counter lubricant.

First of all, your partner should be lying on her stomach with her bottom slightly raised by a pillow. Liberally apply a lubricant (no, spit is not a lubricant) to your penis. Make sure the lubricant is NOT oil-based, like Vaseline—it can cause a condom to break. It is not usually necessary to apply it to her rectum. Position your penis at the entrance to her rectum and slide it in *without stopping* one half or three fourths of the way in. Now take it out. No surprise, this will hurt! It will hurt far less, however, than if you were to slowly insert your penis inch by inch. Think of how cold a swimming pool is when you ease your body into the water and how quickly you warm up when you just jump right in. Some women claim if they bear down (as though they were having a bowel movement), it facilitates the process but I don't endorse this. Anal intercourse can be messy. You are going against the flow of traffic as it were.

Once you have completed your first entrance and exit (and have thereby accustomed the rectum to your penis), you may enter again and proceed with regular thrusting. Women don't have clitorises inside their rectums, I don't care how many porno movies you've seen! Since it's virtually impossible to reach down and stimulate her manually (unless you're facing each other), I recommend the use of a vibrator during, or performing cunnilingus after, anal intercourse. Do not insert your penis into her rectum and then into her vagina, either. The risk of giving her a urinary tract infection—or worse—is high.

This is what women have to say about anal sex:

"It hurt like hell at first. After a while, I really liked it. It made me feel very submissive which is kind of weird but I'd be lying if I didn't admit it turned me on."

"If Karl gets me all turned on and crazy and everything and won't put his penis inside me, I'm usually ready to have him anywhere and that's how we got started with anal sex. He gets pretty wild."

"I hurt like hell and I'm not doing it again."

"I'm too afraid of getting AIDS. There are too many other things I'd rather try than anal intercourse."

"I'll only do it if it's my idea. If a guy tries to pressure me into it, I always say no."

"I told my boyfriend I'd let him do it if he let me strap on a dildo and do it to him. We liked it so much we do it all the time. He'd die if he knew I told you because he thinks people will say he's gay."

THE TEASE

The tease isn't a specific position, it's a technique guaranteed to get her so "sexed up" she can't see straight. Most women have come to expect an established set of behaviors from their partners (okay, we're kissing and here we go with the breasts, etc.). For you to do the unexpected will really get her attention. Remember how exciting sex was in high school? Remember how wild we got because we were never sure what might happen next? Will she or won't she? Will he or won't he? Teasing operates on those same principles.

You can kiss her. You can tongue her to the brink of orgasm. You can grab and squeeze and touch her everywhere but you cannot insert your penis. Oh, maybe you threaten to—teasing her clitoris with the head of your penis or even inserting just the tip—but no further. Uncertainty will whet her appetite like crazy because after all when do *you* play hard to get?

Only when you think you're going to pass out do you finally make ravishing love to her. Or maybe not. Maybe you just drive her wild for a few days.

AFTERWARD

Afterward is just as important as before and during. No, it's more important. She has given you the gift of herself. She has taken your flesh inside her flesh. She has surrendered. The last thing you want to do is roll over and fall asleep.

Women—all women—want to be held afterward.
They want to be cuddled and talked to. It's terribly important that you continue the bond. Ann Landers did a
famous survey once and found that a huge percentage
of women have sex for the express purpose of cuddling
afterward. If that doesn't tell you how negligent most
men are about giving affection and attention, nothing
will.

Sex is both a sublime and ridiculous thing. So last but
not least, it's imperative to keep a sense of humor about
it! It takes time to get into another person's sexual
groove. That's why for so many couples who aren't
afraid to explore each other sexually and emotionally,
sex keeps getting better and better, *not* more and more
boring.

Good sex takes great courage.

16

Technique, Technique, Technique

The second most eloquent instrument on your body—besides that fabulous tongue of yours—is your hands. Your hands are a Stradivarius from which you'll wring the most beautiful melodies. They are bringers of both pain and pleasure; they can slap or soothe. In other words, they are capable of all things.

You, however, being the artist that you are, will elicit the most magnificent and earth-shattering responses with those hands. By manning all the buttons on your partner's control panel, you will send her into galactic hyperdrive. The technique is simple but the results are . . . Well, I'll let them speak for themselves.

You must first of all hold your hand as though you were making a pistol with it—two fingers pointed out, the rest curled under. Now raise your thumb. Then:

1. Place your thumb on her clitoris.
2. Insert your fingers into her vagina.
3. Rest the knuckles of your last two fingers against her rectum. Don't grind, just press.

Making sure her clitoris is well lubricated, slowly twist your fingers in and out of her vagina. Gradually increase the pace. Maintain as much contact as possible with the clitoris itself but you can expect to lose it occasionally. No problem—the lighter the pressure, the greater the intensity of her orgasm. Note: when she does come, very softly flick your thumb over her clitoris, barely moving it at all. During orgasm, a woman's clitoris may disappear altogether but don't let that worry you. With a shudder of satisfaction, it merely snuggles down into the soft pink blossom of itself. Post-orgasm, the clitoris may be ultrasensitive, too sensitive to touch. That being the case, cease all manual stimulation and use your *big* gun. I imagine you'll get a very warm, wet reception.

17

On Becoming a Legend

LEGENDARY TECHNIQUE NUMBER 1

There are few things more blissful than this particular technique when executed properly. The trick is to exert the right degree of pressure at the right time. One woman who especially enjoys this equated it to "body painting with your own juices." The idea *is* the same. And lubrication is the key.

1. Wet two fingers inside your mouth or her mouth.
2. Insert your fingers slowly but deeply inside her vagina. Simulate the rhythms of your penis but vary it—sometimes quickly, lightly; sometimes deeply, forcefully.
3. Now very quickly slip your fingers out of her vagina and slide them over her clitoris. Use a light, fast pressure.
4. Plunge them into her vagina again.
5. Repeat, only this time prolong your contact with her clitoris.

There should be a slick highway between her vagina and her clitoris upon which your fingers swiftly travel. It's the combination of light pressure on her clitoris coupled with the powerful thrusting of your fingers that makes this so exciting. It's unexpected. When you feel her coming, pull out of her vagina and focus—softly, lightly—on her clitoris. Barely moving at all. And once again, the clitoris being the sensitive, delicate organ that it is, don't continue to manipulate it once she's through. Give it a rest. Then begin again.

LEGENDARY TECHNIQUE NUMBER 2

Oh ho ho. Won't *you* be popular after mastering this technique! A more sublime distillation of erotic impulses was never conceived. For her to be truly appreciative of your sexual genius, lay her on her back and spread her legs. You should have an unobstructed view of her treasures.

1. Keeping your tongue hard and pointed, slide as much of it as you can inside her vagina. Move it around—back and forth, up and down, not necessarily in and out. Your tongue, unlike your fingers, is double-jointed, so wiggle it as much as possible.
2. Now keeping your lips away from the clitoris itself and keeping your tongue pointed, "wag" your head from side to side (as though you were saying no). Starting from the vagina, slowly guide your tongue up toward her clitoris and back down again.
3. Insert your tongue back into her vagina. Then make your way to the clitoris, stopping this time to

stimulate it more fully. You should now take your fingers and work them into her vagina while your tongue is stimulating her clitoris.

4. Switch. Now it's your finger that is lightly brushing her clitoris while your tongue is working its magic inside her vagina.
5. Continue switching until she approaches orgasm. Bring her to orgasm with your tongue only. Remember: a light pressure side to side is enough to do the trick.

If you can perform this smoothly, without a lot of forced or jerky movement, all will proceed satisfactorily. Linger at least thirty seconds at each "station" before switching. At the moment of truth, keep your tongue barely twitching on her clitoris and your fingers inside. And watch the fireworks sizzle!

LEGENDARY TECHNIQUE NUMBER 3

In terms of satisfying a woman, nothing takes the place of your penis. Nothing. There's just something wildly atavistically exciting about having one inside that drives every woman wild. It's both a sexual impulse and a procreative one.

Your penis is, for our purposes at least, primarily an instrument of pleasure. So when you are fully erect, try the following:

1. Fully lubricating your partner's vagina, use your hand to press the head of your penis against her clitoris. Try a circular motion as opposed to a side-

to-side motion (or the head of your penis, being hard, will ride roughshod over the clitoris instead of smoothly gliding).

2. Slide it down to her vagina, effect no penetration, then slide it back again.

3. Repeat steps number one and number two several times before actually penetrating her vagina with the head of your penis. Just the head, no further.

4. When finally entering her vagina fully, vary the depths of your thrusts and the forcefulness with which you administer them.

A word to the wise: contrary to previously stated advice, a firm pressure against her clitoris is recommended here. Why? The movement, in order to be effective, must be continuous. Not bumpy. So the more pressure you exert against the clitoris the less likely you are to "skip" across your plane of resistance. This technique will eventually drive both you and her absolutely crazy, so when you're ready to go for the gusto, place your thumb lightly against her clitoris and plumb her depths. No mercy here: really do it like you mean it. It'll be one for the record books.

LEGENDARY TECHNIQUE NUMBER 4

The Seesaw: sex doesn't get any better than this. You will master this one handily providing your aim is true. To wit:

1. If you haven't already noticed (!), there's a very sensitive vein that runs up the underside of your

penis. When your partner is fully lubricated, place
that delicious part of your penis against her clitoris. Thrust up.

2. Now—without using your hands—thrust gently
down into her vagina. Withdraw and thrust up
against her clitoris.

3. Repeat as many times as desired. Most people can
only take so much of this before going completely
insane, so if you start a sexual riot, don't blame
me.

The trick of it is to know exactly where your partner's
vagina is in relation to her clitoris. You want to keep the
rhythm steady and the movement fluid. Don't go bang-
ing around trying to find the thing. Slip it in, slip it out,
slip it up, slip it down. If she's ready to come right away,
press your penis firmly against her clitoris and effect a
rocking motion. You'll know she's happy when you've
got claw marks on your back.

18

How Does She Love Me . . . ?

Throughout history men and women have sought spiritual, physical, and, yes, metaphysical means of making a cherished object fall in love with them. Some struck deals with the devil. Others sought out witches, beseeching them for powers or spells. We gaze longingly into our teacups to determine if the leaves signify a lover. Or huddle around a table with a fortune teller and her Tarot. Most—even those without religious convictions—resort to prayer or bargaining or outright pleading with God or various gods so that they might be sure of securing a loved one's affection. All in all, it's a pretty exhausting process.

And I would be a charlatan of epic proportion if I claimed to possess the secrets for bestirring a maiden's heart. That I cannot do. Nor can I sow the seeds of love in a bosom charred by a lifetime of bitterness, acrimony, or abuse. After all, you will never thaw an iceberg with a blowdryer. What I can do—once you've at least gotten her attention—is help your case along. I'm letting you in on a piece of country wisdom my grandmammy told me and like all grandmammies who have a metaphorical rocking chair and a jug of rye whiskey hid up in the cupboard, her wisdom is golden. "Staci," she said, "Staci, we love the ones we treat good, *not* necessarily the ones who treat us good."

It's a scandalous concept. Because everybody treasures the notion that he or she could love, would love, if only someone feted them with cuddles, kisses, and caviar. Someone who, perhaps, looked a lot like Fabio with his hair combed. And the truth is, I do encourage you to lavish her with gobs of ooey-gooey affection— once you've established a relationship. None of the erotic and romantic acrobatics I recommend should be implemented before you've engaged her heart. No, more subtle yet sophisticated means must be used to pull out her heart and nail it to the wall: you've got to get her in the habit of treating you well.

Women tend to be caregivers. Nurturers. It's built into the system along with breasts and a vagina. But as a rule women don't tender their attentions indiscriminately. They know and are correct in knowing that such gifts are not to be squandered. And by infusing their time and energies into a given arena (namely yours), women realize they are making an investment. An investment upon which they intend to collect. That's why they get so crazy when they've given a part of themselves and you don't respond: they're enraged at you for refusing to honor your psychic debt. No matter, though. Women have long known that when a man pays for dinner, drinks, and a show he's made an investment, too. Not just financial but emotional. He's committed himself to a certain amount of time, money, and attention and likes you commensurately.

So even love becomes a matter of investments. It, like so much else, distills into an exchange of economics— emotional economics. And when you wise up to the reality that men and women are alike in that respect, you'll be one up on the competition. Get a woman to do you a favor and you've got the woman. Whether it's cooking your dinner, looking after your cats, or driving you to the store after you've broken your leg, it doesn't matter. *We like the ones we treat well.* And a lot of men, steeped in masculine self-sufficiency, have a hard time with this. But do it you must . . . if you intend to win this woman's heart. Other favors to consider:

1. Ask her advice about something.
2. Ask her to show you around a new city.
3. Ask for her input on cooking, car maintenance, computers, or any of her fields of expertise.
4. Ask to borrow a food item (and replace it the next day!).
5. Ask her to take your nephew for ice cream while you run an errand that can't wait.
6. Ask her to drive you to the airport.
7. Ask her to run an errand for you.
8. Ask to borrow a book. (Return it.)
9. Ask her to go clothes shopping with you.
10. Do *not* ask her for money.

Sometimes we give the most generously when we allow someone to give to us. Few of us are comfortable, truly comfortable, being on the receiving end. But a well-timed and well-meant thank-you or any other nod of appreciation will go a long way toward setting up an account in LoveBank, U.S.A. Because deep down we have three common denominators: our need to be loved, our need to be understood, and our need to be needed. This latter is especially powerful (it's the one that can keep us in completely dysfunctional relationships with alcoholics, substance abusers, and professional victims). So use this universal Achilles' heel to your advantage: cultivate the art of favor seeking. An added benefit, the message you send by doing so is: I am worthy of your time and attention. I am worthy of this favor. So open your hand. Chances are you'll find hers in it in very short order.

19

You Said It First

How can I tell if a woman is faking an orgasm?

The bad news is, you can't. There are no easily discernible manifestations of a woman's orgasm. Her nipples may not necessarily peak, she may not always get a sexual "flush" over her abdomen. The good news is there's something you can do if you suspect her of faking.

It's what I call "the delayed orgasm." It goes as follows: you say to her one evening that you want to do something extra special. You want her to lie back as still as possible, as quiet as possible, while you give her a good tongue-lashing. The object (you explain) is for her to resist having the orgasm as long as she can (because you read somewhere that it's more intense that way). Why does something this hokey work? Because women fake orgasms for three reasons; 1) they don't want to hurt your feelings if they don't have one; 2) they think you couldn't possibly want to expend the effort it requires for them to have one; 3) they think they have to compete with your last girlfriend who was a huge-breasted nymphomaniacal fellatio queen who howled at the moon every time you had sex. When you play the delayed orgasm game, you are relieving her of the pressure of having to perform. She doesn't have to act. She has enough time to have an orgasm. And she feels like you really must enjoy cunnilingus. This is a much more effective way of handling things than accusing her of faking orgasms!

How important is it to have a large penis?

It's important if you travel in circles where your car, your hair, and your income are more important than your character. If you're determined to play the town stud, having a big penis is probably as advantageous as big breasts are for a woman. Superficial people like superficial things.

Big penises, however, impress men more than they impress women. Big penises are a status symbol—like a hot car, a big income, and a trophy-wife. They do not, however, make you a sexier guy or a better lover. I've never heard a woman say she wanted to find a guy with a big penis. (But I have heard tales of women who, when confronted by monstrous members, packed up their diaphragms and fled. So what's the use of having one if you're scaring women off with it!)

Should we discuss our sexual fantasies?

If it's a fantasy about her—sure. Let her know. Otherwise, keep your fantasies to yourself. Sexual fantasies are private erotic adventures only you should venture forth upon. No woman (no matter how badly she wants to know) likes hearing that you have fantasies about her sister, her best friend, or some sexy movie actress.

What's the best way to initiate sex?

Sometimes the best way to initiate sex is not to initiate
sex at all. Women are funny that way. If you're all over
them like a cheap suit, they don't want it; if you act the
gentleman and give them gentlemanly at-the-door
kisses, they invite you inside. A famous wit once said: "A
woman will never forgive you for not wanting to sleep
with her." So, you don't have to be coy, you just have to
be gentlemanly.

What kind of sexual fantasies do women have?

Women have ravishment fantasies. They have seduction
fantasies with them as the seducer. Some women fantasize about other women. Or sex on horseback. Remember Demi Moore and Patrick Swayze at the pottery
wheel in *Ghost?* I thought every woman in the theater
was going to swoon!

Why do women cheat?

Women cheat when they're neglected. Ignored. Taken
for granted. Women rarely cheat for purely sexual reasons. There's always someone out there who can make
her feel beautiful again, who will romance her the way
you used to. The fastest way to drive your Significant
Other into another man's arms is to be possessive
and/or neglectful. It pays to remember she's a woman,
not just a wife/mother/breadwinner.

What's the best way to end a relationship?

Most women are horrible when it comes to ending relationships. They're afraid to tell you it's over, so they start
getting harder to contact. Sometimes they just keep you
dangling until a rich young doctor happens along. You,

however, will be a GENTLEMAN when it comes time to end a relationship. Instead of not calling her, you will confront her and say it's over. If you have to, tell her you have a Peter Pan complex and you find it impossible to commit. Better still, tell her the truth.

20

What *Don't* Women Want?

Thousands of women (and men, of course) were interviewed for this book. It's amazing how willing we are to discuss excruciatingly intimate details of our sexuality with perfect strangers, yet when it comes to dialoguing with a partner, we shut our mouths faster than a math book.

We all have our eccentricities. For instance, I lecture on human sexuality throughout the United States and Canada, have talked about masturbation on network TV, orgasms on drive-time radio, write on the subject of sexuality, and have many rollicking discussions about vibrators with my friends. But tampon commercials, however, will always make me blush. Sad but true.

Sex, despite the 1970s, is still a dirty word. Many people, however, are quite good at articulating what they *don't* want in bed. Consequently, the following list was compiled from what women told me bothers them most about their sexual partners.

WOMEN ON MEN

1. *He doesn't spend enough time getting me aroused.*

Foreplay, to most men, usually entails kissing with extra tongue, adjusting her knobs, then launching the rocket. While arousal time does vary from woman to woman, most women need more stimulation than this. Since arousal starts between the ears, not between the legs, there are lots of things besides foreplay that you can do to heighten a woman's sexual sensitivities.

2. *He doesn't hold me afterward.*

Snuggling is very important! Women get a lot more out of sex than the thrill of orgasm. There's closeness, comfort, validation, all of which is negated when you roll over and go right to sleep after sex. The bond is what counts here. Brigitte Bardot is attributed with having said that for a woman, sex starts at seven in the morning and ends after she goes to bed. What this means is you can't bury your head in a newspaper at breakfast, go to work, go drinking or bowling with the buddies, drop shoeless and belching in front of the TV at home and then go in, slap your wife on the butt and tell her to roll over. Not if you want a lasting and harmonious relationship! The single biggest misunderstanding men and women have in relationships is in the expression of love. Men think actions define feelings ("I work my fingers to the bone making her happy, providing for our future"). Women think actions and words define feelings ("He never says he loves me"). Women who cheat—or leave—usually do so because they feel unappreciated, taken for granted. Most women will tolerate (almost!) anything except inattention. Don't let romance fizzle in your relationship.

3. He comes too fast/not fast enough.

What's too fast? Don't gauge this on whether she's had an orgasm or not. Women's arousal time varies, remember? You have to determine for yourself how fast is too fast. And don't make the mistake of thinking if you last all night this is going to make you an unforgettable lover. The only thing you'll accomplish is putting your partner in the intensive care unit. One gentleman I interviewed said he drank too much one night, tied a rubber band around his penis (I assume this was to assist him in maintaining an erection), and forgot he had it on until the next morning. When he woke up, his penis had turned an unrecognizable color and he went screaming to the hospital. *Don't* drink and make love. If you want to last longer, keep visualizing the perfect encounter where you perform the way you always wanted to perform. What we can conceive and believe, we can achieve. This is much more effective than thinking about work or baseball scores or visualizing road kills to keep you from getting too excited. What better way to ruin it for you? You might also want to either withdraw completely or stop moving your penis right before the moment of truth, then continue when your excitement subsides. Also keep in mind that women who have orgasms during intercourse generally have them with between three to ten minutes of steady thrusting.

4. He doesn't understand if I say I'm satisfied even when I don't come.

Only in America do we manage to make sex as goal-oriented as business. You know, for many Europeans it is the journey, *not* the destination that is the focus of lovemaking. As I mentioned earlier, women get many things out of sex besides an orgasm. *Most women, in fact, are nonorgasmic some of the time.* Unfortunately, this often gives rise to those agonizing three-hour-long conversations about what went wrong that women will do anything to avoid! So when a woman tells you she didn't come but had a good time anyway, ACCEPT IT. You are responsible for a woman's orgasm—but only 50 percent responsible. The rest is up to her. Should you feel guilty if your partner doesn't climax? Not if you are doing what you can—within reason—to please her in bed.

5. He's too quiet when he comes.

Somewhere down the line, we agreed that women were going to make lots of noise during intercourse. And men were not. Perhaps men were inhibited by the habit of masturbating when there was a little brother sleeping in the next bed or in dorm rooms with dorm mates. Who knows? The men I interviewed said it made them feel ridiculous to make noise during sex. To your partner, however, how you express yourself sexually—vocally—is important. She wants to hear how excited you are by being with her just as much as you want to hear how excited she is by being with you! Don't overlook how arousing groaning, ecstatic cries (even, sometimes, sexually explicit language) can be to your partner.

6. *He doesn't talk to me when we make love.*

Words are everything! As Robin Williams said in *The Dead Poets Society*, the purpose of poetry is to woo women! You, too, will learn the power of language. If your partner has beautiful breasts or hair, tell her. One absolutely gorgeous woman I interviewed said her boyfriend (and previous boyfriends) rarely if ever told her she was beautiful. The boyfriend in question reported that "she heard it all the time from everybody else and he wasn't going to stroke her ego anymore." Bad move. This is the kind of thinking that keeps you dateless on a Saturday night. It's even more important to give encouragement during sex. For example: men's favorite sexual position is woman on top. This is women's least favorite! Why? Women are painfully self-conscious about their bodily imperfections. Being on top makes you feel HIGHLY VISIBLE. Most men don't realize that *in the absence of any feedback, women are apt to think the worst.* While you're having a great time looking at your partner, she's thinking, "I know he's looking at my stomach. God, why didn't I do those sit-ups?" or, "My breasts. There he is, looking at my breasts. I just know he's thinking they're smaller than his last girlfriend's!" That's why—if you want her to be enthusiastic about having sex in certain positions—you have to learn how to give a compliment. Fear is the greatest deterrent to sexual happiness.

7. *He doesn't practice good personal hygiene.*

The longer we're in a relationship, the more apt we are to forget about shaving, washing, and brushing our teeth. We all do it. Little stuff like that makes a big difference, though—especially to women. We have keen noses.

8. *He isn't sensitive to timing.*

For reasons known only to themselves, many men become amorous when their partners are getting ready to leave the house. Or when their partners are asleep. In either instance, your partner is going to be unappreciative of your advances. Too often, the rebuff is taken personally when it was never intended as such. Don't expect women to go wild with passion at six in the morning when she's trying to get to work early to prepare for a big presentation.

9. *He doesn't accept input well.*

Ah, that rare gem, a woman who knows what she wants and tells you! Input is not criticism! Women don't come with instruction manuals, so when your lover makes suggestions to you, don't act as though you know it already. You don't. Every woman is different. I can't say that enough! However, if being "told" to do something in bed makes you feel like less of a man, ask her to "beg" you instead. You might be pleasantly surprised. A lot of couples find this kind of role-playing extremely erotic!

10. *He won't discuss sex, period.*

This is more common than you might think. A lot of men find it enormously difficult to discuss sex with their partner. Maybe they're afraid of what they'll find out! "I like it when you . . ." is a good start to a great conversation. Being shy about divulging personal thoughts on so personal a subject is perfectly and totally normal. I don't believe there's any such thing as obscenity (except for rape and child molesting), but I do believe there are crude ways of expressing sexual feelings. Avoid using the f word and the c word whenever possible (unless it's what *she* says). There are many less offensive substitutes you can use to get your point across.

I also interviewed men on their opinions on women's sexual shortcomings.

MEN ON WOMEN

1. *She just lies there.*

Very, very frustrating. Makes most men feel like necrophiliacs.

2. *She won't talk about sex/won't tell me what turns her on.*

Very common. Fear is a leading factor.

3. *She isn't into oral sex/won't swallow.*

Oral sex is the number one service requested of prostitutes. No surprise—it feels good. More important, the psychological satisfaction is enormous. Despite the sexual glasnost in this country since the 1960s and 1970s, many men still feel that sex is dirty and forbidden. Getting a woman to suck your penis is the ultimate form of acceptance. For some, the thrill is in getting a woman to do something that "repulses" her. Yes, even something as natural as oral sex can be a complicated issue.

You're not a pervert if you like your penis sucked and licked and loved. A woman reluctant to do so is usually afraid (of not doing it right, of you coming in her mouth) or has religious sanctions prohibiting such activity. My advice is not to press a reluctant partner too hard. People get pretty surly when you force them into doing something they don't want to do. But for many women the spirit is willing. If you can communicate without sounding like you dispense sexual advice on a regular basis, suggest she try the following:

1. Use her hand *and* her mouth (hand on shaft, head in mouth).
2. Deep-throating makes many women gag. I don't recommend it.
3. After you do come, it's impolite for her to stumble into the bathroom afterward hawking and spitting. Work out other options. Most men taste okay, nothing objectionable, but if she doesn't want to swallow, that's okay, too. She can let it trickle out of her mouth. Or, if she does admit your penis into the back of her mouth, she'll hardly taste it at all. Or she can stop just before you come and finish the job with her hands, or breasts. Or you can stop and switch to intercourse before you come. Be creative. Proceed with patience.

4. She takes too much time getting aroused.

Yes, sometimes women take FOREVER! There are many ways of heightening a woman's sexual sensitivities before foreplay that will save you from heat stroke. You've read about some already, and there's more to come.

5. She won't initiate sex.

Women widely consider such behavior "unfeminine." Since birth, it seems many women are taught that passivity precedes sexual awakening (Rapunzel, Sleeping Beauty, Snow White, Cinderella). Is it any wonder then that most women are uncomfortable making the first move? A woman initiating sex is the equivalent of a swaggering macho guy taking up needlepoint. Rosey Grier is the exception that proves the rule.

6. She doesn't know if she's had an orgasm.

Men ask, "How can you not know if you've had an orgasm?" A perfectly logical question for them, considering the nature of men's orgasms. However, women have two different kinds of orgasm (and a rainbow of color in between). For some women, it's the "1812 Overture"— fireworks, cannons, and a six-pack of beer. For others, it's a building up of pressure and—a release. There's not a "high" involved necessarily. So if a woman says she doesn't know if she's come or not, she may not be acting coy with you. With all that activity going on, it's sometimes difficult to tell. Or, it may be her way of saying she hasn't had an orgasm and isn't willing to lie about it but doesn't want to hurt your feelings, either. Women are mysterious creatures!

7. She is nonorgasmic.

Most women are not orgasmic 100 percent of the time. Some women never are. Most women also need to have had an orgasm by themselves before they can have an orgasm with you. To further that aim, I advise you to buy her a vibrator and encourage her to use it. Vibrators are the easiest way for a woman to climax. Vibration, however, is not a motion found in nature—nothing you can duplicate with your hands or tongue—so she needs to "graduate" onto a less direct means of pressure: water. A shower massage or simply the water faucet in the bathtub. Once mastered, she can try using her fingers. If a woman can have an orgasm using just her fingers (on her clitoris, not necessarily in her vagina), she can have an orgasm with you. Most women literally have to learn how to masturbate. Hard for you to imagine, maybe. (It's important to point out here that a woman can't see or handle her vagina the way a man handles his penis. Unless she is a contortionist, there's no way a woman can look at her vagina without the assistance of a mirror. Much of a woman's sexuality, therefore, is imaginary. And therein lies the problem.)

All previous how-to manuals exhort you to stimulate a woman's body (like you would a man's), but ignore her imagination. But wise men know, if you want to get into a woman's bed, you must get into a woman's head. That's what makes the approaches described in this book so different. You're learning how to excite her mind *and* her body.

8. She isn't comfortable with new positions.

While she's worrying about her breasts and her cellulite, you're thinking you're the luckiest man alive. Even if she doesn't take compliments very gallantly, it's important to give her encouragement—especially if you want her to feel comfortable and receptive to your wonderful sexual talents and exciting new ideas.

9. *She talks about or compares me with old boyfriends.*

When I hear some of the hideously hurtful things women have said to men (and vice versa), it makes me want to write a whole book on sexual etiquette. Classy people do *not* make wistful references to past liaisons nor do they compare other men's performances in bed—favorably or unfavorably—with that of their present partner. One man I talked to said his last girlfriend told him she was so glad he wasn't "hung like a stallion like my ex—it just hurt so bad!" Ouch! I'm not saying you don't eventually discuss past relationships but certainly not in the beginning of a new one. Don't like hearing about it? Say something! Tell her straight up you don't like it and you don't do it to her. It's almost impossible to emotionally and sexually manipulate someone who's aware of what you're doing and dares to call you on it.

10. *She discusses our sexual relationship with her girlfriends.*

Most men contend that a sexual relationship should stay in the bedroom. Well, maybe it should but an awful lot of men engage in graphic "locker-room" conversations themselves. The paranoia stems from their belief that women sit around comparing penis sizes. And some do, no doubt. But while many men speak generally about their sexual experiences ("We did it EIGHTEEN times last night," "She was BEGGING me for it," "We're talking VAST TRACTS OF LAND here!" "I bent her over the sink and let her have it," etc.), many women speak about their feelings ("He finally told me he loved me," "I felt kind of empty inside after we made love," "It's so strange to be with somebody after Bob," "It was the first time I've had an orgasm with a man," etc.). Women talk about a lot of things and sex is usually one of them. But hopefully, you're with a woman whose taste and discretion you can rely on.

11. *Women say they want Alan Alda types, "sensitive" guys, but they really want Clint Eastwood tough guys.*

No. What women really want is a man who can be sensitive without compromising his masculinity. What does that mean? It means she wants you to do all your "guy" things—buying tools, fixing cars, burping beer—*but* she wants you to be able to talk about feelings occasionally. She wants you to remember her birthday and your anniversary, to say "I love you" from time to time. She's not trying to turn you into some mama's boy! She doesn't want one. But if women can buy tools, fix cars, and burp beer, men can learn how to ask a woman how she *feels* about something. It's not that complicated.

12. *Women use sex as a bargaining medium.*

Some do. But some men are also guilty of thinking a woman's sexual favors can be bought. If you can only gain sexual satisfaction from your partner after you've gone into crippling debt to please her, you're just as much to blame as she is. Move on.

21

Q&A, Revisited

Dear Staci:

I've been seeing Sherri for about three months now and we get along really well. The only problem is (or is it a problem?) she hits me up for money. Constantly. I help her with her rent, her car payment, her insurance—you name it. On top of which she's always asking me to buy her clothes and pay for dinner. Sherri has a good job but whenever I ask her what she does with her money, she gets super-defensive, even angry. Staci, I'm starting to feel kind of used. What do you recommend?

Pete S., San Angelo, Texas

Dear Pete:

Gosh, it's so hard to be practical when the heart yearns, the penis aches, the palms sweat at the very mention of her name! Is this money you can afford to lose? If so, who cares? Write it off under "entertainment." If not, you've got a problem. You see, whether Sherri is using you or not, she has a big hang up with money. To her, love IS money. Maybe she had a daddy who neglected her but bought her expensive presents. Maybe you have underlying feelings of worthlessness and think you only deserve a girl like Sherri if you pay for her. Who, after all, can divine the mysteries of the human heart? But motives aside, Pete, I strongly urge you to reassess the relationship if you plan to deepen your level of commitment. They don't have debtor's prisons anymore but you'll be looking at years of financial ruin if you allow her greater access to your heart and your wallet. With women like Sherri, the spending always escalates. Always. And as you know, the best acid test for the sincerity of her affection is refusing to spend that kind of money on her anymore. Good luck.

Dear Staci:

I'm short, I'm bald, and I weigh, tops, 135 lbs. I'm obviously no Adonis. But does that mean I'm doomed to dating ugly women? I guess if I had a ton of money, things would be different. As it is, all the good-looking women I want to date won't date me.

Alan J., Houston, Texas

Dear Alan:

Probably because they sense—and rightly so, Alan—that you don't want to date *them,* you want to date the way they look. Who needs it? If they were willing to settle for a superficial relationship, they might as well get involved with wealthy men (just because they're wealthy), or gorgeous men (just because they're gorgeous). As it is, you offer them nothing in the way of love, caring, commitment, or conversation (how could you when you're so busy appraising them physically?). Get with the program and find a woman to fall in love with. Leave your ego outside, Alan baby, because frankly it stinks. And I promise as soon as you stop pursuing women to gratify your underfed ego and start pursuing women because of their worth as human beings, women will respond to you quite a bit differently. It does, of course, entail some emotional risks, which you've avoided operating under your current assumptions. It's easy to blame your problems on the way you look. After all, how we look does play a part in who we get. But I've seen too many beautiful women with homely men (who weren't even rich, thank you!) to put that much merit in your pet theory. Sorry, Alan, but you're the superficial one, not the women you want to date!

Dear Staci:

I'm Jewish and my fiancée is Catholic. Is there any hope for us? So far our differing religious beliefs haven't been a problem. I've heard so many horror stories though, that I find myself worried. What do you think?

Jonathan Z., New York City

Dear Jonathan:

Well, the bad news is I don't know too many couples who've done this successfully. Especially when there are children involved. So if your intention is to eventually warm a nest, I would say a little prayer, do a little dance, and try to keep the relationship conflict-free. Because all too often power struggles ensue over the question of faith.

There are methods of solving the problem. Agreeing beforehand in which faith the children will be raised isn't one of them. (The deferring partner invariably changes his or her mind.) Taking the children to temple *and* to church ("Well, Zoe and I think the kids should decide for themselves") does tons more harm than good because the kids feel pressured to make a decision—a decision I might add that will alienate at least one beloved parent. No, the solution may lie in as great a sacrifice for the general good as you've ever made: a nondenominational church. Not everybody is capable of making that kind of concession. But all too often conflicts over religion become the focus of a host of ills. (We have only to observe world history to remember this.) Ultimately, you must ask yourself what is more important: the children having spiritual guidance even if it is nondenominational, or raising them in a specific faith that will, nine times out of ten, cause terrible tensions at home? Perhaps even divorce? For even those who take their religious duties lightly before marriage often change when the baby arrives. Beware, be smart, and good luck!

Dear Staci:

I really like this girl I've been seeing but she's still involved with her old boyfriend. She says she's going to break it off with him but she's yet to do it. Her excuse is she doesn't want to hurt him. I'd like to get closer to her but how wise can that be considering our circumstances? Any advice?

Glen B., Timonium, Maryland

Dear Glen:

That's such a tired old refrain, isn't it? "I don't want to hurt him!" Blech. Yet who does it ultimately hurt? You! This, Glen, is one of those awful times you'll have to search your heart and ask, "Would I honestly like this girl so much if she were completely available?" Some women are smart enough to know that triangulation (you, her, and the illustrious third, her boyfriend) is the fastest way to ensnare your interest. Nine times out of ten, however, what the woman tries to accomplish by keeping the lines of communication open with her old boyfriend is a place for her to run in case things between you two don't work out. She's also smart enough to know your interest may wane once she's yours. It's a gamble. So really question your motives here. After all, while true love is rare and precious, there are other women out there who are emotionally unencumbered. It may behoove you to find them. She may also be using you to manipulate her boyfriend's flagging appreciation, to elicit a wanted behavior in him, or to make him jealous. I'm also suspicious of people—men or women—who spend undue lengths of time with their exes. It signifies lingering attachments that, while perfectly understandable, spell disaster for new loves. Glen, you're obviously enamored of this woman so my advice (which is to shed her like old skin) will probably go unheeded. Therefore, I exhort you to go into this thing with your eyes open.

Dear Staci:

I'm thirty-two, married, and I have a son and a daughter. My wife is attractive but I've been trying to get her to lose the weight she gained during her last pregnancy. When she's this heavy, I'm just not wild about sleeping with her. Worse, I've fallen in love with another woman who works in my office and am considering a divorce so we can be together. I've had affairs in the past but I've never been in love like I am now. What do you suggest I do? I'm really torn.

Myron W., Tucson, Arizona

Dear Myron:

First of all you have my sympathies. Yours is not an easy place to be. Whatever googly-eyed ideas we may harbor about having simultaneous romantic entanglements, it is never easy and rarely enjoyable. However, taking responsibility for your unfaithfulness is crucial to your making the right decision here. As tempting as it may be to make your wife's chubbiness the reason for your straying, by your own admission you've had affairs before, presumably when she wasn't chubby. This indicates that the problem is yours. It stands to reason then that you cheat not because your wife is unattractive but because of some deep-seated need on your part. In fact, the majority of men who cheat do so for reasons of ego, not sex. To prove to themselves and others that they've "still got the stuff." Unfortunately for you, you fell in love. And that complicates matters.

If I were you, I'd set a deadline for when you were going to make a decision—say three months from now. Until then I advise you to exercise extreme discretion in your affair, promising nothing, and wait and see. If after the initial excitement is over and you still want to forsake your family for this woman, go ahead. Personally, I happen to think kids are a whole lot more important than that, but judging by the actions of others I am in the minority here. I will say this, however: kids are extraordinarily sensitive and unless you want your son to grow up to be some kind of womanizer, I urge you to rethink your penchant for cheating. Children pattern what they see. I wish you luck and unclouded judgment!

Dear Staci:

You're not going to believe I'm writing to you about this but the source of all the friction in my current relationship is: music! My music! I really like heavy metal and acid rock but Pam, my girlfriend, likes jazz. Whenever we drive somewhere and I put a tape in, it makes her crazy. At the house she starts yelling if I play something like AC/DC. What gives? I'm ready to wring her neck.

Dave P., Milwaukee, Wisconsin

Dear Dave:

On par with most couples, the source of friction in your relationship isn't any one particular thing (the toilet seat, the toothpaste tube, whatever), it is power. Who's got it and who's gonna get it next. We all do it—witness the many times we wage epic war over petty nonsense we can't even remember after the dust settles. No, Pam may not enjoy listening to heavy metal or acid rock (and in all fairness to her, Dave, acid rock *is* a specialized taste), but were she in the first throes of love with you, she would probably find it less intolerable. When love ripens past initial infatuation, when it becomes apparent that our merged selves are still separate, we often find it hard to "forgive" the other person. We assign blame for our feelings of irritability and disappointment to the faults, real or imagined, of our lover. It is part and parcel of a maturing relationship. Pam would be wise to realize this; however, you must recognize, too, that by playing acid rock or any loud aggressive music you are erecting a barrier of sound that creates a distance between you. It is virtually impossible to be intimate or to enjoy the loving communication women so dearly cherish when AC/DC is blasting out of your speakers. You, Dave, need some distance, which doesn't mean seeing less of Pam but enjoying more things by yourself. Take up jogging, for instance. And for heaven's sake, get some headphones! In the car, ask Pam what she would like to listen to. In the 1950s, the Soviets used loud music to torture dissidents (we did the same thing in this country to the Branch Davidians), so don't torture Pam with music that drives her to drink. Imagine yourself being forced to listen to ten hours of polka music and you'll begin to understand!

Dear Staci:

I'm pretty frustrated. Not only is my wife unresponsive in bed but whenever I suggest we do anything the slightest bit out of the ordinary, she freaks out, calls me a pervert and won't talk to me for days. I want to stay married to her—she's the mother of my children and I love her—but I'm starting to feel awfully sorry for myself. It seems like everybody except me has a fulfilling, exciting sex life. I don't know how much more of this I can take.

Wayne T., Louisville, Kentucky

P.S. She's always been like this, even before we were married. I guess I thought she'd get over it.

Dear Wayne:

Any cop who takes down eyewitness accounts of a crime knows that different people will see the same event in completely different ways. You and your wife see sex from different perspectives and you are feeling wronged and misunderstood. I commend you for hanging in there. Deep-rooted anxieties attach themselves barnaclelike to sexual issues, making them much bigger than they actually are.

First of all, Wayne, you need to ask yourself is this sexual scenario something you really want or do you just want it because she won't let you have it? In other words, is it a control issue or a sexual one? Remember how much neater other kids' toys looked than our own? Nothing's changed! We still demand certain things of our spouses so we won't feel deprived. Barring those circumstances, it sounds to me like your wife is rather inhibited. Counseling may or may not help depending on whether her inhibition stems from a strict puritanical upbringing, childhood sexual abuse, or some other traumatic shame-inflicting event that stunted her development. I would advise you first to read Chapter 9, "Bodytalk," and, using those guidelines, let her open up to you. A word to the wise, however: don't ever browbeat, badger, or bully a woman into having sex. Even if she capitulates, the resentment will be thick enough to cut and serve for dinner. If all else fails, you yourself must find a counselor to talk to (ideally you and your wife would attend together) so you can sort through your feelings of anger and frustration. Good relationships are never easy!

Dear Staci:

My girlfriend and I have nothing in common except for our genuine attraction for each other. When the dust settles, how long can that last? I'm old enough to know these things don't go on forever.

Robert S., Boise, Idaho

Dear Robert:

Good question! That would depend entirely on how fast you chew it up. A couple who see each other every day for three months is burning the fuse pretty quickly. On the other hand, a couple who put some distance between their encounters is going to experience the kind of infatuation that leads them into making ill-judged decisions (such as "My God, I must love her—let's get married!"). The absolutely worst thing two people can do together is sanctify what is truthfully a sexual attraction by calling it something else. The unfortunate thing about a high-octane attraction is that the disappointment when it wanes leads to some heavy-duty fighting, hurt feelings, anger, hatred, and revenge. Does that mean I don't advocate combustible sexual attractions?

No! They're a wonderful reminder that you're alive. So have at it, Robert. Just remember when the end comes to try to do it with grace.

Dear Staci:

I know this sounds awful but I'm really really attracted to my best friend's girlfriend. She's smart, sexy, and has a body to drive any man insane. Sometimes when things aren't going so well between her and Doug, I get the feeling she likes me. Am I a total heel for falling in love with someone who—morally—is strictly off limits?

Pete S., Baton Rouge, Louisiana

Dear Pete:

Are you honestly in love? Because if you are, you have my sympathies. Sometimes we think we've fallen in love with someone who's off limits when all it winds up being is the lure of forbidden fruit. Another old classic: two men fighting for the same woman. And fight you will if you indulge this dangerous passion. It's not an "if" but a "when." Frankly, I'd cool off and take a long hard look at your life as it is right now: Are you locked into the same dull routine? Are you meeting enough new people, women especially? Are you happy with your work? Because when we crawl into our bottle and add the cork, folks we wouldn't normally look at twice start to look pretty good. That much is inevitable. My advice, Pete, is to make the effort of broadening your vistas socially for a while. Then if you still have feelings for your best friend's girlfriend, make your decision only after you've exhausted other resources. Don't fall prey to erroneous thinking like "We'll only do it once and get it out of our systems." Once done, you'll be in it up to your elbows, old boy.

Good luck.

Dear Staci:

I've never told anyone this before, but nothing—not the most beautiful girl in the world—turns me on like seeing even a plain woman wear black stiletto heels. We're talking major excitement here. I guess what makes me feel bad is that the woman wearing them is incidental to the shoes themselves. I'm sensitive enough to feel like I'm using her. I guess you could call it a fetish although just seeing the shoes doesn't excite me anywhere near as much as seeing them on a woman's feet. What do you think?

Felix H., Hobbs, New Mexico

Dear Felix:

I commend you on your sensitivity! And you're right— the woman *is* incidental to the shoes themselves. That's the bad news. The good news is that any woman who senses the passion she *or* her shoes arouses in you is a lucky woman. Not all men are capable of great passions, be they for shoes, ideals, or women! So count yourself among the lucky few. As long as you take pains to assure your partners that it is they whom you wish to see wearing the shoes you have no reason to fear hurting their feelings. Your only cause for concern, Felix, is if you are incapable of performing sexually without them. If that's the case, counseling is advised. If you prefer the shoes but can function quite well without them, then it's not a problem. The guilt you feel can be minimized by knowing that any sexual passion (unless it involves coercion, violence, or children) is a splendid thing.

Dear Staci:

I'm a really affectionate guy and, unlike a lot of my friends, I like being affectionate in public. Unfortunately the girl I'm with (who's a knockout) isn't affectionate with me. It makes me mad because I want people to know we're together. Am I demented or is this a legitimate gripe?

Frank G., Toronto, Canada

Dear Frank:

Congratulations! I receive tons of mail from women who are disgruntled because their husbands and lovers won't demonstrate any public affection! You're one in a million. However, it sounds to me like in your present case, being affectionate with your sweetheart has less to do with spontaneous expression and more to do with "Hey, look everybody! I bagged this babe!" By your own admission it makes you mad because you want people to know she's yours. Sadly, Frank, few things turn a good-looking woman off more than having some guy all but pee on her to mark "his territory." It skews the relationship. Instead of devoting his energies to keeping her in the relationship, he is wasting his time keeping others out of it. It's ultimately self-defeating. So I caution you to exercise some restraint. You'd be surprised by how quickly some people will come to the table if you back off. But you must maintain that distance in order not to scare them away again. It's often difficult. I'm not advocating any chilliness in your manner, just neutrality. If you achieve this balance, you won't have to worry about other guys moving in on your relationship because *she* will make it clear that her heart's engaged.

Dear Staci:

It went like this. One day at soccer practice I saw my friend Mike making out with a girl who was not his girlfriend and I got pretty mad. Trisha's a wonderful woman and deserves better. Stupid me, I decided to tell her and between Trish crying on

*my shoulder and my caring for her, we became lovers. Now I'm
really in a quandary because: 1) I'm no better than Mike (except that my girlfriend doesn't know); 2) I'm in love with
Mike's girlfriend; 3) Mike would lose his mind if he knew. I
can't believe this is happening to me.*

Steve J., Edison, New Jersey

Dear Steve:

Well that's quite a Peyton Place you've described there.
And you're right about one thing: you're in a steamin'
heap o' trouble! Your first mistake of course was telling
Trish what you saw. Under those circumstances, it's always best to steer a wide berth. Your second mistake was
to express your tender concern for her feelings in a sexual manner. But your greatest and most heinous crime
was to sit in judgment on your friend. Were you privy to
his heart? How do you know he doesn't love this woman
and wasn't planning to break it off with Trish before you
blundered along? Remember that adage about glass
houses! Steve, I can give you advice but instinct tells me
you will follow the path of least resistance: Mike will continue to secretly enjoy his affair and you and Trish will
sneak around behind his back. Ultimately Trish will
break it off with you when Mike finds out (she'll make
sure he does) and you'll be savaged by hateful emotions
watching them patch things together again. Consequently, your girlfriend will either get really angry or
blow you off altogether and you'll be left holding your
you-know-what in your hands. It's been done before,
compadre. What you should do, of course, is break it off
with Trish, tell Mike the whole story, taking full responsibility for what happened, and hope for the best. If
your girlfriend finds out, you'd better deal with that,
too. Handled correctly, I think there's a good chance

your friendship will come out intact. So do the right thing, Steve. Good luck.

Dear Staci:

Well, where do I start? My mother hates my wife. It isn't an emotion I suspect her of secretly harboring. Oh, no. I know she hates her because she tells me so on a daily basis. Now they're not talking to each other. Last week I guess Mom told Jennifer once too often how to raise our seven- and ten-year-olds and Jennifer called her expletives I dare not mention here. I love my mom. I love Jennifer. But what should I do?

Morris J., Virginia Beach

Dear Morris:

Divide and conquer, Morris, divide and conquer! It sounds to me like your mom is way too involved in your life. First of all, you need to put some distance between your wife and your mother. Have them take a breather. Second, you need to get it fixed in your own mind that you're a grown man and your wife and family come first. It has to be this way. Otherwise, you'll be a little boy all your life, too emotionally dependent on the wrong woman. Third, you must sit down with your mother and establish some ground rules: 1) you will no longer tolerate her incessant bad-mouthing of your wife; 2) she is never to offer unsolicited advice about the children; and 3) each ensuing offense will be paid for by one week's banishment from your house. Period. You can expect your mother to cry, scream, withdraw into an injured silence, make you feel guilty, and threaten to kill herself. Mothers have many weapons, sophisticated and crude, in their arsenal. Frankly, Morris, the first time she started flapping her gums about your wife you should have laid down the law. Now matters promise to be more difficult. But it must be done! So put on your flak jacket and enter the fray. If you owe your mother anything, it's the chance to be a better person. Jennifer has to cooperate, too, and refrain from complaining about your mother.

Dear Staci:

I know this is the twentieth century and all but I'm worried I masturbate too much. After all, how much is too much? I'm between girlfriends right now and I must do it three or four times a day. Does that make me a compulsive masturbator? No, I'm not afraid I'm going to go blind, but I do suspect an aberration.

Jeff B., Butte, Montana

Dear Jeff:

The only cause for concern that I can see is not the frequency of the masturbation itself but the way you possibly masturbate. If you grip yourself too firmly you may wind up "spoiling yourself" for the real thing. In other words, regular intercourse may not offer you the same degree of intense stimulation that your hand does. I warn women who use vibrators about the same thing. I therefore advise you not to use a "death grip" on your penis but proceed gently. If the frequency of your masturbation is starting to affect the way you live or is dictating your personal habits (like whether to go to the store), then you may have a problem. If you're addicted to masturbation, one orgasm may be to you what one drink is to an alcoholic: you can't stop. Should that be the case here, counseling is advised. Otherwise enjoy your ability to enjoy yourself and hope for better romantic prospects in the future!

Dear Staci:

Does having fantasies about being with another guy make you gay? From time to time I think about it and—guiltily—enjoy it. It's got me really worried. Please tell me I'm okay and not some homo. I'm petrified.

Tom A., New Carrolton, Maryland

Dear Tom:

You need to examine what scares you so much about being "some homo." But know that a huge number of straight people have gay fantasies. Gay men often have straight fantasies. But that's all they are: fantasies. Just because I fantasize about climbing Mount Everest doesn't mean I'm going to scale that killer wall in my garden. Your fear is what's causing your distress, not the fantasies themselves. So let's address your fear.

First of all, what makes a man gay? One homosexual experience? Two? Five? Twenty? I know lots of otherwise straight men who experimented with homosexuality in their teens. After all, we all have to have a sexual outlet. But in my opinion, that doesn't make anyone gay. Many people believe we are all inherently bisexual. The most common fantasy men have—two women making love to each other—is believed by some experts to be the conscious expression of men's unconscious homosexual impulses. It's all relative. That's why I don't want you to worry that you're a mutant because you have gay fantasies. First of all, being gay isn't a disease or anything to be feared. And having gay fantasies doesn't mean you're gay. It means you're human. So lighten up. And please don't let your fear manifest itself, as it too often does, in loathing and hatred of openly gay men. *That's* ultimately self-destructive.

Dear Staci:

I just can't stay monogamous. It's not possible. I try and I try but women come on to me all the time. You only go around once, right? I think it's too much to expect for two people to stay faithful all their lives. After a while, stagnation sets in. The only difference between me and other men is I do what they only dream about.

Jeff D., Houston, Texas

Dear Jeff:

You may be right. Perhaps it's impossible to stay monogamous all your life without drying up sexually. But I don't believe that. The man or woman who reaps the rewards of a safe, secure relationship while cheating on the side is trading in cheap betrayal. So if you know you can't stay monogamous, don't break your (wife's?) heart by only living the charade of a commitment.

Frankly, I'm suspicious of any man who says he has a compulsively wandering penis. I begin to question whether he strays for sexual reasons or merely for the conquest. If it's just good sex you're after, you can find good sex with one woman. But if you feel deep-seated insecurities by bedding woman after woman you'll never feel better about yourself. Not in the long haul. The unhappiest people in the world are people who have something to prove: the woman who flirts to prove she's pretty, and the man who uses his penis as a barometer for how big a stud he is. So don't be a jerk, Jeff. Don't make nice with the ladies while pretending to be a one-woman man. It's ugly. And if you're causing a whole lot of women a whole lot of pain, I advise you to rethink your actions and maybe get some therapy. After all, as you said yourself, "You only go around once."

Dear Staci:

I'm probably the only guy in America who has this problem, but I can't come when a girl gives me head. It doesn't even get me all that excited. I much prefer making love to oral sex—giving or getting. Do I have a hang-up? I know Samantha would prefer it if I really got behind that stuff, but I don't. Most guys would kill for a girl who enjoyed it and here I am, a real bump on a log. Help!

Mickey P., Bangor, Maine

Dear Mickey:

Hey, either you do or you don't. In terms of your own dissatisfaction with having her perform fellatio on you, don't worry. You're not abnormal. A lot of men don't find it that exciting. And a lot of men do! Just because I like apple pie, for instance, and you don't doesn't mean you're abnormal. So judge yourself less harshly. And try keeping an open mind.

As far as Samantha goes, are there other things she enjoys as well? Perfect them! But I've got to be honest with you, Mickey: you eat it, you own it. Was there some traumatic experience in your past that prevents you from expressing your sexuality this way? Important question! Equally important, you must tell Samantha your reluctance has nothing to do with her. Otherwise, women are apt to think they smell, they're not doing it right—you name it.

There's a big difference between reluctance and repugnance, hmm? Figure out which one you feel and act accordingly. If it's the former—well, sex is a two-way street. Sometimes we go the extra mile to make our partners happy. The latter? I'd be willing to bet either fear or ignorance is hampering you. Should that be the case, go to the library and learn all you can about female sexual organs. I'm serious! Study up. After that, the whole issue of oral sex will seem less scary.

22

Impotence

It's a fear that's commensurate with a tax audit: impotence. Unfortunately, it strikes virtually all men at least once in their lifetime. And no amount of pleading, cajoling, licking, stroking, or fantasizing will make the thing stand at attention. If anything, your lover's anxious blandishments make it worse! Compounding the issue is a sickening realization that you've let two people down—yourself and your partner. Plus, you have a witness to your humiliation.

Many factors induce impotence: booze, medication, a lost job, a physical condition or a psychological one. If impotence is chronic and there's no physiological cause, you may harbor deep-seated fears of your mother or rage at an ex-wife. More than any other reason, however, financial problems, getting fired, laid off, or being passed up for a promotion will conspire to make you less than a stallion in bed. But while the majority of women understand and empathize with occasional impotence, few will take meekly to outright sexual neglect. It perplexes a woman why, when all else is going to hell in a handbasket, the one pleasure available to you (namely her) is so rudely rejected. Little do they understand that for most men—possibly yourself—being strapped financially equals complete and total emasculation. And when problems arise in the bedroom they tend to permeate the entire relationship. Hence, the high divorce rate among couples after a husband's lay-off. It's a sad but vicious cycle. And all too often the man starts drinking, which—if he had an initial problem with impotence—seals his sexual doom.

Not a pretty story, is it? But all too common. Being sexual—especially being romantic—is tough when you're under the gun, but unless you want a belligerent boss, ungrateful kids, *and* a disgruntled wife, it's best to make the effort. So if impotence should occur from time to time, don't panic. Stay calm. Above all, don't try to force it. Your penis is telling you something (and when, my friend, has it ever lied?). It's saying, "No, thanks, not right now." You wouldn't force an unwilling woman to have sex, so why would you force your penis? The main thing I advise is to tell your partner that it isn't her fault, that both you and your penis find her very attractive, but that he's gone on strike for the moment. Over a labor dispute, perhaps. A woman's primary anxiety when your penis malfunctions is that she personally wasn't woman enough to get you excited. Ironic, isn't it? You're in a cold sweat because you can't get excited to get her excited and she's chomping her nails to the quick worried that she's incapable of getting you excited to get her excited. Life. Someone should sell tickets.

Do not dwell on occasional impotence as though it were a death sentence. It will pass. If, however, you have a physical problem or are taking medication, you are advised to see your doctor. You'd be amazed by how many prescription drugs conspire to cripple you sexually.

The use and/or abuse of alcohol will almost certainly

impair your sexual performance, as it makes it virtually impossible to achieve or sustain an erection. Among younger men, alcohol may have a reverse effect: priapism, or the inability to ejaculate even though hard. This isn't good either because after ten minutes of steady thrusting, your partner's vagina is going to look like raw hamburger meat. My advice is to eschew alcohol altogether, or at least when you plan on being sexual. And the same goes for drugs. Even pot can have a deleterious effect on your sexual performance.

If time passes, no physical problems are detected, and you still have difficulty achieving or maintaining an erection, I recommend you visit a good therapist. Your penis and your heart (the heart symbolizing the seat of your emotions) are not separate entities; it is therefore wise to have your mind, as well as your body, assessed professionally.

In terms of your immediate problem, which is *her* sexual needs, remember the many techniques detailed in this book. Sometimes alleviating your penis of its requirement to perform is just enough to get it going again! So concentrate on giving her pleasure. It is good to exercise your other organs—to say nothing of your imagination! Above all, you must be patient with yourself! Your penis may be attached to you but it often works its own agenda, so treat it—and yourself—with kindness and respect.

23

The 101 Best Places for a Quickie

There's nothing like a quick session somewhere naughty, don't you think? The following list is a compilation of places couples have made love. Women often fantasize about semi-public sex . . . easy for them not to worry, you say, because they have internal genitalia. True. But that's no excuse for you to not walk on the wild side! Even if you *do* get caught, you'll discover that it's not the end of the world. The truth is, most people are far too self-involved to care what you do with your penis. What a liberating realization! So muster up some courage and enthusiasm. It'll be an experience neither of you will ever forget!

1. In your mother-in-law's bedroom.
2. In a cemetery at night.
3. In a canoe, under the stars.
4. In a hammock.
5. On or under the dining room table.
6. In the sleaziest motel in town.
7. In the men's room of a Chinese restaurant.
8. In a back alley downtown.
9. In a movie theater or a drive-in.

10. The dressing room at a lingerie store.
11. The bathroom of a gas station.
12. Getting fellated under a table with a long table-cloth.
13. In a school bus (after hours, please!).
14. On a deserted nature trail.
15. In an airplane bathroom.
16. In the backyard when it's raining or snowing.
17. Over the pool table.
18. At the local lovers' lane.
19. In the parking lot of your local government building.
20. In the back bookshelves of the library.
21. Under the bleachers at a football game.
22. After hours at work.
23. After hours at work, on your boss's desk.
24. In the foyer, first thing coming home.
25. In the back seat of your car.
26. In a gazebo.
27. In an empty stadium.
28. In the back of a Ford pickup.
29. In the bathroom sink.
30. In a bathtub full of Jell-o.
31. In the broom closet of any public building.
32. In a storm cellar.
33. In one of the private rooms at a tanning salon.
34. On the fire escape.
35. In a private box at the opera.
36. In the coat closet at any boring office party.
37. On horseback.
38. Getting a hand-job under a trenchcoat on the bus.
39. In a deserted swimming pool.
40. Under a deserted pier at the beach.
41. In the port-o-potty at an outdoor concert.
42. On a porch swing.

43. In the locker room *well* after the game.
44. In the parking lot of your local police precinct.
45. In a small impromptu ice cave.
46. The bathroom of a fast food restaurant, mall, or bowling alley.
47. On the roof, under the stars.
48. Inside a parade float.
49. In your neighbor's tool shed.
50. One hundred miles out in the middle of nowhere.
51. In a horse-drawn carriage.
52. Outside in the mud.
53. Backstage. Anywhere.
54. On stage (without an audience).
55. In an elevator, between floors.
56. On a swing set.
57. In the back seat of a taxicab or a limousine.
58. On the lid of a grand piano.
59. In an inner tube going downriver.
60. In the laundry room of an apartment building.
61. In a store front window after hours.
62. On any piece of city construction equipment.
63. On the stairs.
64. On a Ferris wheel.
65. In a pair of gravity boots.
66. Straddling an OB-GYN table, a dentist's chair, or a weight bench.
67. Between two parked cars on a car lot.
68. In a pup tent in your living room.
69. On a rubber sheet with a bottle of baby oil poured over you.
70. In a deserted part of the reptile house at the zoo.
71. In a coffin or a hearse.
72. In a hay loft.
73. In a hot air balloon.

74. In a baby's playpen.
75. Beneath the golden arches, after hours.
76. On a secured ladder.
77. While wearing the same huge pair of pants or overalls.
78. In a hospital bed.
79. Stuffed in a closet with a hundred balloons.
80. On the diving board of your neighbor's swimming pool.
81. Anywhere at your old high school.
82. In a treehouse.
83. Any enclosed bus stop.
84. Underneath her enormous hoopskirts at a Halloween party.
85. While rolling down a hill together slowly.
86. In a bathtub full of grapes, peeled or otherwise.
87. In a phone booth.
88. On abandoned railroad tracks.
89. In the stairwell of an apartment building.
90. On a balcony with a dozen wind chimes.
91. In somebody else's Winnebago.
92. In a "think tank"—a sensory deprivation tank filled with saline.
93. On top of a bar after hours.
94. In a Jacuzzi—especially when it's thirty below outside.
95. In the trunk of a Cadillac (lid open!).
96. In the show room of a neon art gallery.
97. On a ski lift.
98. In a penthouse with a panoramic view of the city.
99. While snorkeling underwater.
100. In the sleigh that takes you through the haunted house ride.
101. In the footwells of the back seat of your car . . . while parked in front of the 7-Eleven.

24

The Ultimate Challenge: Sex and Parenthood

After the blessed event, expect your sex life to go right out the window. No ifs, ands, or buts. Not only is there an enforced physiological sexual hiatus post-partum, but it's highly unlikely your wife's going to be keen on any hanky-panky at all. Not with one ear cocked toward the nursery. You see, guys, this monstrous maternal instinct kicks in, which, along with a sudden depletion of hormones, makes it impossible for some women to even hear the word "penis" without screaming. It's all a part of Nature's Plan to regulate the frequency of a woman's pregnancies. If you were to zap her right out of the gate, she'd have no time to recover her health and her strength. There is only so much assaulting one womb can take.

So kick that sex drive into a lower gear, amigo. Now is the time for you to be ultra-attentive and romantic without being sexual. Be patient. Soon you'll find a sitter and take your sweetheart out for a night on the town. It is especially important that you reassure her of her own attractiveness now. Not many women feel like heartbreakers after giving birth! For some reason society desexualizes mothers and it's not going to help you any if she feels less feminine.

Sex during pregnancy, while not the wild-eyed, sheet-ripping variety, can be sensual nonetheless. It will probably be easier for her if she lies on her side during intercourse. Unless her doctor advises against it, there is no reason to abstain during pregnancy. In fact, many women find it very, very sexy! So don't desexualize your wife when she's pregnant—enjoy her in the full blossom of her womanhood. And remember that after the baby arrives, spontaneous sexual expression will be difficult. So plan ahead!

25

The Breakup

Men do several interesting and ritualistic things when getting over a relationship:

1. Drink till they puke.
2. Find anyone or anything that will have sex with them.
3. Shave all existing facial hair.
4. Grow a beard.
5. Watch ESPN till their eyes bug out.

It never fails.

Far be it from me to cramp your style. If you want to down half a bottle of Jack, go ahead. But the pain's still going to be there in the morning. Along with a humdinger of a headache. Not to mention a pair of panties flung suspiciously over the lampshade—panties that belong to someone whose name you can't remember. The fact is, getting over a relationship hurts. Your heart feels pain. No, you are *not* invincible and if someone cuts you, you bleed. Even if you instigated the breakup, you are surviving the loss of a love and will have some heavy-duty healing to do. Hopefully, you'll learn something about yourself along the way.

Recovering from a bad relationship, or even a good relationship that somehow ran out of steam, feels terrible. You may also feel angry, numb, irritable, restless, or guilty. Or all of the above at the same time. Sundays will be excruciatingly painful but the best thing you can do for yourself is admit you're hurting. Many people are afraid to give free rein to hurt; the pain *can* seem bottomless. But it isn't. Pain has a floor that, even when you're free-falling, your feet will find. And the more time you spend with your hurt, the sooner it will go away.

Healing takes time—small solace to those who are frantically trying to backpedal out of heartbreak. And healing isn't a smooth acceleration from zero to sixty. It's full of stops and starts just like learning to drive a stick shift. Sometimes you stall out altogether and try to salvage the wreckage of your old relationship. Don't. Attempts at reconciliation are, for the most part, sloppy ways of avoiding your pain. And for heaven's sake, whatever you do *don't* pull the jealous lover routine by spying on her to see who she's dating. Don't freak out if you see her lip-locked with another man. Don't call and hang up. Don't obsess. It belittles you and you'll look like a fool. Understand that the rage and jealousy you feel at the thought of your sweetheart in some other guy's arms is standard price at the box office. Everyone pays it. That doesn't mean you get to act like George Foreman with an attitude.

It's perfectly acceptable to feel angry at: 1) yourself; 2) her; 3) the new man in her life; 4) your parents for having given birth to you; 5) society. Anger is fine. It's really important to remember, however, that the way you express your anger determines your level of maturity.

Do not: 1) scream at anyone; 2) kick the dog; 3) slash your wrists; 4) do any structural damage; 5) beat someone senseless. Pain is not a license to be a jerk. That's what racquetball is for. And should the question of suicide arise, know that the thought (not the act) is a natural outcome of heartbreak and that you are not alone. Lots of people consider suicide (only a few actually do it). If you're afraid, however, that the thought of doing away with yourself is getting out of hand, *seek professional help at once*. Call the operator and ask for the local suicide hotline. A woman I know promises herself and others that whenever she wants to make friends with a knife, she'll postpone doing it until the week after. By then, most things look a whole lot better.

Your sales resistance is going to be at an all-time low so avoid making any major purchases. And since nature abhors a vacuum, the chance of your getting involved with someone unsuitable is very high. Don't. When the new relationship goes south, you'll have *two* heartbreaks to mend. And who's got that much glue?

Now is the time to get involved with people and hobbies, classes and activities. Go parasailing with friends, or camping or hiking (unless, of course, you shared those same activities with her). Don't try to see how many pizzas you can consume in one sitting. In weathering this crisis, you can expect a certain amount of self-destructive behavior but don't let it get out of control.

And sometimes when you least expect it, the sadness will clutch your heart again. You'll hear a certain phrase that reminds you of her, a song you shared, or find her hair ribbon in the back of the closet. It doesn't mean you're starting from zero again. Recovery is an incremental process—*always* two steps forward, one step back. So lick your wounds and move on.

In your anger and confusion, you will be tempted to

use and abuse some sweet unwitting woman like (you're thinking) you yourself were used and abused. Such as waiting until after you've had sex to tell her you are incapable of making a commitment. Or crying on her shoulder about your ex (totally tacky). Or sleeping with her, then "forgetting" to call. How can you expect to be legendary with that kind of track record?

Remember, "That which does not kill us makes us stronger."

When you salve a wound with alcohol, it stings. So it is with your pain. Let it hurt for a while. Let it heal. Trust that the pain will pass and when it does, love will embrace you again.

26

Mean and Green: Dealing with Jealousy

Jealousy has more to do with *your* feelings about yourself than it does *her* feelings about someone else. Plain and simple. But it remains, along with grief, one of the most galling and painful of human emotions. Jealousy is different from envy in many important respects. Webster's, for instance, defines "envy" as "a feeling of discontent and resentment aroused by contemplation of another's possessions, qualities, or achievements, with a strong wish that they were one's own." By contrast, the word "jealous" is described as "fearful or wary of being supplanted, apprehensive of loss of position or affection." To covet something is bitter enough, but to fear emotional demotion in a loved one's heart—aye, there's the rub. Why does jealousy prick us like a thousand pins? Obviously rejection demoralizes the healthiest egos. But more significantly, it spits in the eye of our most robust fear: that we were judged and found lacking. That we were ousted in favor of someone younger/richer/better-looking. It daunts us on so many different levels, it's no wonder some people respond by trying to inflict as much suffering on others as they themselves are experiencing. Of course they end up suffering more themselves. Penny, a thirty-three-year-old medical assistant, told me:

"I couldn't stop driving by his house. It humiliated me but there I was night after night, waiting, watching. I didn't have a plan, just a compulsion. It was horrid. My routine went as follows: I'd come home from work, shower, put on fresh makeup and drive to our old apartment (where Mike continued to live). On the way I'd pick up a burger. I'd just sit there and eat it, watching. It was a miracle I got anything down at all, I was so sick to my stomach. Nerves. I was terrified of getting caught.

"One night I just couldn't sleep. I kept tossing and turning because I knew, I just knew he was with someone. I got out of bed, threw some clothes on, and drove over to the apartment. Sure enough, about three minutes later he drove up and there was a woman with him. And here's what's so amazing. When I got a good look at her and realized she wasn't attractive, I was furious. Don't get me wrong, I'm sure I would have been furious if she was attractive but this I couldn't understand. It flew in the face of logic that I was cast aside for a woman whose butt was the size of a coffee table. I was aghast. To make matters worse, I crept up to the door and listened to their lovemaking. I would rather be gnawed on by pit bulls than go through that again. I was continuously drunk for the two weeks following that little episode. I had to take vacation time to do it. And to this day I have no idea why I was so jealous of Mike. I've had better-looking, sexier, more jet-setty boyfriends. But none that drove me to such dark and desperate deeds. I pray to God I never experience anything so painful again."

Penny's story is far from uncommon. Jealousy is a universal emotion. The problem is most people won't discuss it—as though uttering the word could summon the very demon of it. It is important, though, to note what

Penny said: "I have no idea why I was so jealous of Mike." Of course she doesn't. But closer examination reveals that Mike stumbled into Penny's life during a time when she was feeling awful about herself. Penny's real dream was to be a doctor, but when she met Patrick, her husband, she postponed medical school so she could work and put Patrick through law school. When their marriage ended in divorce, Penny was inconsolable. In her mind, both her career and her marriage were abysmal failures. Shortly after that she met Mike. Now Mike became the focus of her anguished love and frustrated ambition. And Mike, sensing this, quickly withdrew. Penny's self-worth, unstable to begin with, went into a free fall and she found herself in the throes of a humiliating compulsion: to find a reason, any reason, why Mike left. And when the reason proved unsatisfactory (i.e., the woman, in Penny's mind, was less attractive than she), Penny anaesthetized herself with alcohol for two weeks. After which she went into therapy and gained some perspective on herself and the relationship.

So that's why all those old saws about self-worth, having your own identity, being your own best friend—while tiresome—are true. Because when you slacken off in those areas, the Green-Eyed One is right around the corner, chortling. And being in love, of course, makes it all too easy to forget to take that language class you've always wanted to take, or go to the gym, or continue your tai chi. Love is the most potent drug you can get without a prescription. It's no wonder people experience such appalling withdrawal symptoms when the stuff is taken away.

In assuaging a jealous woman, it is wise to cuddle, coddle, and (gently) correct her mistaken assumptions about where you've been spending your time. Up to a point. If she has a maniacal *unjustifiable* jealousy and it's getting out of hand, however, you're wasting your time trying to appease her. Insist she talk to someone about her uncontrollable feelings. Because after a certain point it is no longer your problem. It is her problem. And if it continues to affect the relationship (and your peace of mind), you'll know she has some serious self-esteem issues to tackle.

But sometimes when a woman is jealous of a man, other factors enter into play besides her self-esteem (or lack thereof): your emotional availability. It's a sad but all too common phenomenon that a man, once comfortably ensconced in a relationship, ceases to verbally communicate. In the beginning he instigates three-hour-long phone conversations, talking about everything from his dog to his first erection. After a while, though, familiarity puts vise grips on his tongue. His conversation consists mainly of information, not emotional exchange. And his woman wonders: "Where did it all go wrong?"

Then she begins to speculate. And her speculations go something like this: He's emotionally unavailable to me because he's emotionally available to another woman. Or because I don't have big-enough breasts. I don't interest or excite him anymore. He's not in love. Therefore I'm going to: a) nag him into an early grave (but at least I'll get his attention); b) leave; c) have an affair with someone who will talk to me; or d) work it out. Meanwhile you'll be kicking back a few beers and watching the playoffs, completely unaware that any turmoil exists. Until you hear the clicking of her suitcase . . .

So besides being just the right thing to do, communication (talking about feelings, yours and hers) becomes necessary to her own peace of mind. And ultimately yours as well. That's what you can do to allay some of her jealousy. Be sure that your behavior isn't causing her upset, either. Remember that ogling women, remarking on their anatomy, or sharing that sexual fantasy you have about her best friend is a definite no-no. Trust me—as flattering as you may think it is to have some woman eating her heart out over you, you don't want it. It'll haunt you like a bowl of bad chili. Because when a man is jealous, he tortures himself. When a woman's jealous, she tortures *you.*

Which, conveniently enough, brings me to my next point: you. Your jealousy. From what I've seen, men have a harder time with it than women. Richard, for instance, nearly went insane:

"Beth and I were an item for close to five years. We lived together, planned to marry, blah blah blah. Then I met Sandra and that was it. She was every man's fantasy, sexy beyond belief. I started seeing her on the sly and Beth found out. Needless to say, she wasn't happy. So we split for a while and I continued to see Sandra only it wasn't like it was before. I guess she only liked it when I wasn't available because she kind of left me for a rich married guy. I'm sure I deserved it after being such a heel to Beth. In hindsight I realized that getting married—married to anyone—was scaring the shit out of me. That's why I took up with Sandra.

"About six months go by. I kill myself trying to get back together with Beth. I call her, send her flowers—I would have walked to hell in my underwear to be with her. It's funny how sometimes you don't realize you love someone until after they're gone. But Beth, she doesn't want any part of me. And one night I'm at a restaurant and I know why. She's found another guy. Some weenie who used to model or something. Well, I just flip. I'd been drinking a little and I caused this big scene, threatening to beat the hell out of the guy. I can see that Beth is completely embarrassed and I'm so glad. I wanted her to suffer. As for the guy, he just stares at me like I lost my mind or something.

"The next night I drive past Beth's house at two A.M. and Beth's car isn't in the driveway. Same thing the night after that. Now I'm not getting any sleep and my work's starting to suffer. The third night I see two cars in the driveway—hers and a Porsche. Something inside me snaps. I got my baseball bat out of the trunk and smashed that car to smithereens. I even slashed the tires. And the lights in the house come on, dogs are barking, and Beth and her new boyfriend are half naked on the porch, staring in disbelief. Pretty soon I hear the sirens and I make to get out of there only Romeo up there flying-tackles me. We struggle. I get in a few good licks. Then the police break it up and haul my butt to jail. I'm still paying for the damage to that car. And Beth took out a restraining order against me. Couple months ago I heard they got married. The feeling, the jealousy, is less intense than it was but I don't think I'll ever be totally over it."

Richard describes that episode as the low point of his life. Ironically, though, he set himself up for it. Because nine times out of ten those who are the most jealous are those with the guiltiest consciences. It just works that way. They project their faithless impulses on their partners. If you yourself have a roving eye and find yourself consumed with jealousy for your wife or girlfriend, you need to rethink your own behavior. Several men of my acquaintance are married to gorgeous, intelligent, sexually uninhibited women upon whom they habitually cheat—not for reasons of sex but for reasons of ego. And they're insanely jealous. Eventually they'll get caught. Maybe one, maybe two will have the courage to seek counseling and salvage the wreckage of their relationship.

Biology figures significantly in your experience of jealousy. It is your biological predisposition as a man to want to perpetuate your genetic legacy without interference from other men. It is the natural way of things. So you might reasonably expect to feel the sting of jealousy on an occasional basis. A little jealousy is not a bad thing. But if you find yourself in the jaws of an overwhelming case of it, take a good look at your life and a thorough inventory of your soul. Chances are you're feeling deficient in some area. That's the part you want to change, not your partner's personal freedom. Unless of course you have legitimate cause to be jealous. In which case I suggest you hash it out with whatever party or parties are involved. But my prescription is still the same: do something for yourself. Get involved with a charitable organization or take a class. Join a club or cultivate a hobby. Fill in the huge bite mark Jealousy left behind when it tore a chunk out of your confidence. And realize that time—and only time—will heal your wounds.

27

Six Sexy Ideas to Help You Win Her Heart

1. If you're uncomfortable saying "I love you," write it on a paper airplane and sail it over to her. Any naughty suggestions are terrific, too!

2. Buy her a package of boudoir photographs featuring—herself! Photographers are selling packages at very reasonable prices. If it makes you feel any more comfortable, retain the services of a female photographer. What more artful way to tell her she's *your* calendar girl! Just don't surprise her with a photographer and a heap of costumes. Make sure in advance that she's into it, too.

3. After sex—especially if you happen to end up in a "spooning" position—many women find it incredibly romantic when their partner falls asleep after some tender cuddling with his penis inside them.

4. If money isn't too great an object, rent space on a billboard she passes on her way to work and send her a public love letter. I guarantee she'll go right into romantic orbit (or maybe off the road!).

5. Surprise her one day by hiring a masseuse to come in and give her a good rubdown. It's so much more relaxing at home and a lot of legitimate masseurs/masseuses make house calls. Take her out to dinner afterward, then go home and see what ELSE develops!

6. One man I interviewed, a very romantic man whose newlywed wife can't say enough wonderful things about him, planted an engagement ring in a box of Cracker Jacks. When she found it, he knelt down and proposed.

28

A Gentleman's Guide to Buying Lingerie

Many a man has made the mistake of buying the item of lingerie he would most like to see his lover in only to have it retired posthaste to the back of her underwear drawer. "Where did I go wrong?" they wonder, scratching their heads. The secret to buying your lover lingerie she'll wear is buying your lover lingerie she thinks will camouflage her "trouble" spots. If she believes she looks like a pregnant whale there's little likelihood you're gong to get her into a body stocking!

That's why I've made a list of recommended items for different figure types. More than how she actually looks must be taken under advisement, however: you have to consider how she feels. If she's constantly harping about her hips or stomach—even though they look as tempting as watermelons in a hot July to you, find something that will cover or flatter her hips and stomach. I advise you go to a retail store where the saleslady (who understands perfectly what you're going through) can steer you in the right direction.

Slim Women/Small-Medium Bust

A slim woman looks good in just about anything. Look for bodystockings (usually a sheer or mesh stocking that hugs her body neck-to-ankle) or browse through the selection of bra-and-garter sets. If you decide to purchase any garter set you need to buy crotchless panties or panties with side ties. Why? It can cramp your style if, in the heat of the moment, you have to undo each one of her garters to get her panties off. If you buy "easy access" underwear, you have the added benefit of being able to make love to her while she's wearing all her pretty things.

Bigger Women/Medium-Large Bust

Ask your saleslady for a look at the merry widows. Merry widows are great for fuller-figured women because they're like corsets with built-in bras. They come with garters, so once again you'll have to raid the crotchless panty section. Pretty lace waist-cinchers accentuate a fuller figure, too, as do most things that nip in at the waist. If you're purchasing anything with a bra, pilfer one from your lover first. Don't count on a woman telling you her true bra size or your remembering it. The best thing to do is bring the bra with you.

Women Who Hate Their Thighs

This is a woman who'll like the way she looks in a teddy. A teddy is a one-piece that goes from her neck to her thighs and should snap under the crotch. Get one that's loose-fitting and it'll effectively cover her tummy. If you're ever in doubt, sexy, floor-length nightgowns cover just about every trouble area she has.

The same rules apply when buying costumes. Rethink that "Sheena, Queen of the Jungle" outfit if she has a problem with her body! Of course, if she likes the idea of sexy lingerie, or exotic costumes, use the opportunity to prove to her that *you* know there's no problem with her body.

29

Women's Fantasies

The following are excerpts from interviews I conducted with women of all ages, nationalities, and socioeconomic backgrounds. Where appropriate, I have substituted certain words or phrases. What truly fascinated me was the degree to which—even in their fantasies—women have sexually empowered themselves. The woman-as-seducer theme, once relatively rare, is now common. More remarkably, no fewer than ten women reported having fantasies about men making love to men—not unlike men's fantasies of women with women. Women, however, seem to make an enormous distinction between what they want in a sexual fantasy and what they want in a man. In other words, in reality they expect a man to be the aggressor. Oddly enough, many claim to want to initiate sexual intimacy but sense that men felt emasculated by their aggression! Ironic, isn't it? Here you are ready to give your eyeteeth for a woman like that and they're all busy doing the "Who, me?" routine.

I included this chapter because of the secrecy that enshrouds not only women but their fantasies as well. It is not intended to make you feel like a starving man star-

ing into a restaurant window. Some fantasies described
are powerfully erotic, some sensual, others mere flights
of fancy. Not included are fantasies described to me by
women whose earliest sexual memories were violent and
whose fantasies are therefore violent. Those would be
the subject of an entirely different study.

Marlene, 32, is a marine biologist:

"My life's work is the sea and since childhood I grew
up next to it, every day, every night, the sea. No wonder
my sexual fantasies involve diving or snorkeling or being
on a boat somewhere with nothing but the sun and the
water and the seagulls crying. I'm out there every day
and it never fails to give me a rush.

"The only thing I've never done is scuba in the buff.
I've always wanted to. In this particular fantasy I'm off
the Florida coast, alone, and except for my gear, completely naked. The water is magnificently clear and blue.
I can feel the thrill of it against my skin, the satiny
smoothness, see the coral glowing and the bright fish
darting ahead of me. Then in the distance I see something else. A man. He, too, is naked. How he looks
never changes. Of course he's impossibly handsome and
masculine but his hair is dark, a little past his shoulders.
It undulates in the current. And since we're underwater
words are impossible. We swim toward each other and I
know immediately what he wants and he knows I want it,
too. There's no doubt or hesitation. But this is where it
gets weird. He has no breathing apparatus and now neither do I but we're still able to breathe. Like I said,
weird. And he enters me immediately, forcefully, although the water makes his movements fluid. Everything's suspended, dreamlike, unreal. Even the feel of
his body is altered by the water and behind me the sea-

weed tickling and above me the sun on the water. It is such an awesome fantasy. We're able to kiss, he sucks my nipples, everything. When I come he comes and the water's churning like crazy. He kisses me again and I swim away. I have variations on this fantasy. Sometimes fish brush past my clitoris or I meet my lover in a grotto instead of underwater but the feeling's still the same. Water is another world, an alternate reality. Life began in the ocean."

Randi, 28, is a human resources manager:

"I feel kind of strange discussing this. I mean, fantasies are so private. Especially something as raunchy as this one. Oh, well. My favorite fantasy involves two men and myself. Okay, okay, my boyfriend and his brother . . . God, I feel so guilty. So Mike, my boyfriend, and I are naked on the couch, just starting to mess around when Steve walks in. At first, everybody feels awkward, but then Steve puts his hand between my legs. Mike sees this but it turns him on so he starts kissing me. Pretty soon Steve is eating me out and Mike moves up and puts his penis in my mouth. Sometimes I don't make it past this part but other times I think about Mike eating me out while Steve does me from behind. Or in my ass. There, does that shock you? I told you I'm depraved! It's hard for me to be around Mike and Steve sometimes I want it so bad. I mean, if I found out Mike wanted *my* sister, I'd kill him."

Tammy, 46, sells office equipment:

"I have this kind of outer-space fantasy, I guess. Pretty far out. It involves a faceless man. Strange, huh? I mean I can't see his face very clearly. It starts out like a 'zipless' encounter but it gets a lot more intense because right above his penis there's a tongue! I'm being completely serious. So while he has his penis inside of me the tongue is going crazy on my clitoris. I know that sounds bizarre. Few things get me more excited than thinking about it, though."

Leeza, 22, works for the Postal Service:

"My favorite fantasy is very detailed and specific. It involves a pizza delivery guy I've never met but I know he's out there somewhere! He's tall, about six foot one or six foot two, with streaked blond hair. He's got really broad shoulders and narrow hips. And this particular day I order a pizza so he has to come to my house. When he rings the bell I answer the door wearing a pair of really short shorts and a halter top. I can tell he's really digging it. He comes in to give me the pizza but when I go to pay him I realize that I don't have enough money for a tip. He says, 'That's okay,' and starts to go but that's when I reach under my halter top, pull out my breasts and say, 'Wouldn't you like these for a tip instead?' He kind of smiles and his breathing gets kind of quick and shallow and his eyes darken. I unzip his pants, fall to my knees, and give him incredible head but he wants to do me instead. So he spreads my thighs apart and goes to town. We do it doggie-style sometimes or with me on top. It depends. I always imagine that afterward he comes to my house delivering pizza whether he's got a pizza or not!"

Sheryl Ann, 38, is a cosmetic sales representative:

"I have this vision, really. Well, it comes to me like a vision or like something that happened to me a long time ago. Another lifetime perhaps. There isn't any sex involved really but to me it's very very sexy. It's a sultry summer night in Mexico and the town square is strung with lights and paper lanterns. A carnival is about to start. Everyone's dressed in Mexican costume, the women wearing skirts and the men wearing loose white shirts unbuttoned at the neck. Then the music really heats up and the dancing starts. I'm standing there watching when this incredibly sexy Mexican approaches. He's tall and lean and wears a thin mustache. Without a word, he whisks me away and we dance with ever-increasing passion. At first he kisses my open palm. Then my throat, my lips, the fabric covering my breasts. Everybody's intent on doing his own thing so no one notices. Pretty soon he's grinding his pelvis against mine, gyration after gyration, and that's usually when I come. I find the anonymity of it very exciting. I love the free-spiritedness of Mexican culture."

LaMara, 24, works in pet care:

"My best fantasy involves going to dinner with this guy that comes into the store sometimes. He's never asked me out or anything and I know he doesn't know I like him. He kind of looks like Billy Dee Williams. Well anyway we go to dinner at this really fine restaurant and after we finish eating, I excuse myself to use the ladies' room. The men's room, I can see, is down the hall from the ladies'. When I come out again there he is just standing there grinning at me. We start to kiss slowly at first, then really passionately and he pushes me through the door of the men's room and into a stall. He does it to me from behind. I'm loving it but sometimes some guy will walk in and we'll have to keep quiet. Then he'll go to town on me again. I love the idea of semi-public sex but I haven't been able to find anyone brave enough to try it with me yet!"

Catalin, 29, is a chemist:

"Okay, here's my biggest slut fantasy. I'm a reporter in the men's locker room after a big football game. The team won and the guys are pumped. You can feel their energy. I'm interviewing this really sexy guy—you know the type. Beefcake Central. Big blue eyes, baby-boy face, muscles of Death. Pure masturbation material. And he's really putting out the vibe for me. I can't stand it so after it's cleared out I come back and he's there alone putting stuff away in his locker. Before even kissing me, he rips my skirt and panties off and starts eating me out. You can imagine how absolutely wild I'm going. Then he raises up and fucks me for all he's worth on the bench. But that's not the end of it. Eight or ten of the other players come back to pick him up for their big celebration and when they see us together, a couple of them get pretty excited. Pretty soon they're all taking turns fucking me, one after the other. That's fairly explicit and impersonal, I know, but that's what gets me excited."

Rowena, 30, is a piano teacher:

"I guess because I'm in music, I fantasize about musicians. Not classical musicians, but really die-hard rock 'n rollers. Bad boys. My favorite fantasy involves being a groupie and getting backstage. I imagine myself doing the lead singer or sometimes the whole band."

Heidi, 56, is an inventory manager:

"I almost always fantasize about encounters I've had in the past. There was an airline pilot once who for some reason really did it for me. I felt I could be very uninhibited around him. He was also very sweet and romantic. I wonder where he is today and if we were to get together, would it be as good as it was before?"

Fascinating, isn't it, the scope and breadth of women's fantasies? In terms of their sheer rawness there's nothing there that would indicate any sexual reticence on the part of women, is there? I recorded scores of others that were equally explicit—rarely did I ever sense shame from the women describing their fantasies. Embarrassment, yes, lots of embarrassment, but not the "Oh, God, I'm a sick pervert" feeling I got from many men describing their fantasies. That indicates to me that men are both encouraged to display sexual aggressiveness and inculcated with a sense of their own depravity all at the same time. "Be sexual but if you are, you're a disgusting pig." On the other hand, women are not encouraged to be sexual in the first place. I can't help but wonder how different life would be if we accepted the fact of sex like we accept the facts of eating and sleeping. I know there'd be a lot less sickness in the world.

30

And Now for Something Completely Different

THREESOMES

A lot of men, married or otherwise, fantasize about making love with more than one woman at a time. Better yet if the women experiment with each other sexually while he watches or, perhaps, participates. I contend that many men have terrible fears of sexual inadequacy, of not being able to please a woman. Two women is not only one more of a good thing, it relieves him of the pressure to having to perform. In the age of AIDS, none of the following wilder activities is safe. If you participate, condoms are a must.

Here are some quotes from couples who have experimented with "threesomes" (two women, one man, or two men, one woman).

"I was the one who wanted to do it. My wife was pretty shy about it and felt funny about my calling my old girlfriend, who's bisexual. It's strange how different things are in reality. I mean, my fantasy was 100 percent better! As it turned out, my wife really got into Denise (the ex-girlfriend) and I felt totally excluded. Sure, I got it on with them but I knew they liked it better between themselves. Now my wife wants to see Denise by herself sometimes. I've read that this isn't uncommon among women who experiment sexually but it still makes me feel awful. I thought it would turn me on but it just doesn't anymore."

"We loved it. We're doing it again as soon as possible."

"We'd done it with another woman, but now my girlfriend wanted to do it with a second guy. I'll admit it turned me on to think about me and a buddy putting it to her. What I didn't count on was how weird it was to be that close to another guy with a hard-on. I didn't want to do it with him or anything but it was almost . . . well, homosexual. Of course, *she* loved it. I wanted her to have a good time, sure, but I didn't want her to *love* it. Now it's all she talks about and it's pissing me off."

"I talked my boyfriend into it. I'd always wondered how much better it would be with another woman and he sure was game. My girlfriend and I put on this little show, dressed up, acted sexy . . . you know. But it was still kind of weird. Not at all like I'd imagined. Maybe we weren't drunk enough. But I don't think all the alcohol in the world could have made us less inhibited. I felt like I was just going through the motions."

"It was much better as a fantasy."

"We did it. I divorced her two months later."

Almost everyone I talked to said it was better as a fantasy. No one, however, said they regretted doing it except when it led to breakups or divorces. No matter how emotionally equipped the couples I talked to thought they were, each reported being surprised by the jealousy, the anger, and the fear they felt afterward.

Advice

If you absolutely must experience a threesome, I recommend you do it without your primary partner. Separately, in other words. And I insist you wear a condom. Is that cheating? Well, what's a threesome then? It's often difficult for partners to watch each other enjoying other partners. I'm also very suspect of something that usually entails your drinking yourself to death beforehand.

ORGIES

The following quotes are from a former doorman of Plato's Retreat, a (now defunct) orgy palace in New York.

"Most of the women were pros. I didn't see too many regular girls going there. A lot—and I mean a lot—of high-profile guys doing some weird shit. They had everything—Chinese sex baskets, whips, hip boots—you name it. The thing most guys don't think about when they go to these wingdings is that not everybody there is going to be straight or look like a movie star. The fellas get real freaked out when some homo taps 'em on the shoulder. What's so funny is the hookers who made the most money were the ones who let you do 'em in the ass."

When I asked the doorman if he thought those people were having a good time, he replied:

"I don't know. It never looked that way. They all get this weird glazed look like they're deeply stoned. And nothing ever seemed to satisfy them. I mean really satisfy. I think they just wanted to see how many women they could dork. The only guys who got their rocks off were the ones getting whipped and pissed on."

Advice

If you ever get the opportunity to attend an orgy and you really want to go, don't go with your primary partner. The common wisdom says it'll ruin it for you watching her do the wild thing with some guy in the corner. Some people can handle it but how do you know you're one of them? And please . . . WEAR CONDOMS!

B&D

Lots of couples participate in a little B&D (bondage and discipline) now and again. It's the ultimate tease. It sometimes involves a little role-playing (your withholding sex and her begging for it) or role-reversing (her tying you up and you begging for it). You can lash her ankles and wrists to the bedposts with rope, stockings, handcuffs, or leather straps. You can blindfold her. You can apply different textures and make her guess what they are.

Advice

Tie her up with her silk stockings facedown on the bed. Give her a massage with baby oil and rub your body over hers. Whisper unspeakable things in her ear.

You can do anything your little heart desires because YOU'RE the master and SHE'S your prostrate subject. The idea is to tease her until she begs you to finally make love to her. You control the whens and hows of it.

SPANKING

"My boyfriend and I were joking around one day, you know, just being silly. When I turned to leave, he gave me a little spank on the behind. Trust me, no one was more surprised than I was when I got wildly excited. I made him take me right there on the floor—you know, doing it from behind—and I asked him to spank my bottom a little. I thought I'd just lose it right there! Now he does it on a regular basis and our sex life has never been better."

Advice

A lot of women reported sexual fantasies about being spanked or had actually engaged in spanking games during sex. Hitting is not spanking. The idea is to give her little spanks and bites and pinches where it's most tender. Tell her she's been naughty. Don't be grim about it—have fun.

S&M

I interviewed several practitioners of S&M (sadism and masochism). Strictly speaking, sadists are people who are sexually aroused by inflicting pain and masochists are people who are sexually aroused by having pain inflicted on them. There was a woman in Houston I spoke with who not only had a pricey cocaine habit but a case of tiny razors she liked being lacerated with during sex. Robert Mapplethorpe, the famed photographer, said that S&M wasn't about pain, it was about trust: you had to trust your partner to take you to the edge and not push you over. That may be true. Most people, however, think it's about pain!

Advice

We are the sum total of our memories. Sexually, once you've crossed the line, you can never go back. It's like trying to regain your virginity. The drawback you should be most aware of when experimenting with S&M is that S&M (like crack and heroin) *can* be highly addictive. If you become addicted to the services a dominatrix provides, for instance, going back and having "normal" sex can be difficult. It's hard to get all that excited. Of course, the same thing can happen to people who watch too many porno movies or who masturbate compulsively. Too much of anything can dull the most ravenous appetite.

VIDEOS

The best way to get sex in its proper perspective (and to realize once and for all how inherently ridiculous it is): try having sex on videotape. Watching yourself have sex will tax even the best sense of humor. It's like an X-rated Theater of the Absurd. Still, most people report that it's just as much of a turn-on as watching porno movies you rent from the store. The reason I recommend you make your own is a similar argument I gave about magazines like *Playboy* and *Penthouse:* many women (even those who got wildly turned on by watching porno movies) say they find it insulting to think their partner gets turned on by watching other women. Yes, there it is—that goddess mentality again! But think about it. How manly do *you* feel with all those huge penises throbbing on the screen!

Advice

Make sure you decide beforehand who gets custody of the videos in the event of a breakup. If you're planning to run for Congress—well, maybe I wouldn't do the video at all!

FANTASY ROLE-PLAYING

"My husband and I like to play sex games but I wanted to try something different. So I bought him a Robin Hood costume and me a Maid Marian. He looked wonderful. The only problem was he looked like my husband in a Robin Hood costume—not Robin Hood. And I wasn't any more convincing as Maid Marian. We couldn't keep from laughing, which turned out good anyway because we had a lot of fun. I think we do better playing roles as opposed to doing costumes."

"I'm a car salesperson and so's my wife. Sometimes we go down to the store after hours and I pretend to be the salesman and my wife pretends to be my customer. We flirt. After a while I start to fondle her and pretty soon we wind up doing it in the back of a pickup somewhere. We have a lot of fun with it."

Advice

Fantasy role-playing is for people with good senses of humor. Stay light with this one. Above all, ensure complete and total privacy for you and your lover. You don't want this one splashed all over the "National Enquirer."

TOYS

Toys are fun. Visit your local sex toy retailer and have a blast looking over the selection. Vibrators, anal vibrators, penis rings, French ticklers, "tittie-lube," edible underwear, leather items—you name it and you can find it somewhere. Toys are fun because they make you laugh! And to laugh—especially about sex—is to experience a whole new form of intimacy.

Advice

Some men (perhaps yourself) feel very threatened by toys. They would rather not compete with any appliances they have to plug in first. I assess their feelings to be: "Vibrators? Heck, no! If she has an orgasm, it's going to be one I gave her." Okay, so that's not super-progressive thinking, but there are plenty of other toys to enjoy. I'd hope, however, that her sexual enjoyment might preempt your bragging rights.

31

Fifty Fabulous Ideas for Driving Her Wild

1. Make a date with your Significant Other in . . . the back seat of your car! If you're only parked in the driveway, that's okay. There's one rule, however: you've got to make out a long time before proceeding any further. The more evocative it is of the excitement you felt in high school, the better!

2. Murder Mystery Dinners. If you (like most people) find it a challenge to role-play, you might find it easier to do so within a context. Marguerite Swanson, who hosts Murder Mystery Dinners at Durham House, a Houston-based bed & breakfast, says that sitting down to supper with five other couples in costume, a script in hand, is the best way to become less inhibited. Obviously, a *murder* mystery isn't in itself a prelude to romance, but it can get you and your lover in a totally different frame of mind. Perhaps, a little later behind closed doors, a wildly passionate one!

3. Have you ever camped out in your own backyard? If not, pack up your gear and set up your tent! You

can tell stories, sing songs, roast marshmallows. Set up a teepee instead and do your own X-rated version of cowboys and Indians.

4. Since the whole purpose is to help her shrug off her shopworn, workaday self, it helps to get her into another reality. And the best way to accomplish this is to afford her opportunities of slipping into "a different skin." Most states, for instances, are visited by an annual Renaissance Fair, so if she has a secret hankering to dress up like a wench or a lady, this would be the ideal place to indulge that fantasy. Be outrageous! If you can muster the courage, dress up yourself. And don't worry, you won't be the only guy there who looks a freak in tights. Remember that it's just this kind of role-playing that will help her escape her usual mental status and be all the more receptive to your amorous advances later.

5. Are you a budding author? If so, sharpen your pencil and write a sexual scenario featuring the two of you. Be explicit but *don't be crude!* "Penis" and "vagina" fall much softer on the ear than . . . well, other words you could use. Unless, of course, she insists those words excite her. If in doubt, err on the side of good taste. Always. And when you're finished, read it to her in bed. Women are aurally stimulated so the sound of your voice sliding over those deliciously naughty episodes will have her panting for more!

6. I talk to too many women who complain that their boyfriends and husbands don't take them dancing anymore. It's become such a familiar lament that I started asking men why this was so. I never did get a

satisfactory answer but instinct tells me embarrassment plays a large part in their reluctance! If this is true of you, I have a suggestion that should satisfy you both. One day I want you to clear the living room of furniture, set up a glitter ball or at least some colored lights, rent a tuxedo, and—when she comes home, say, after a hard day at work—greet her at the door with roses and a smile. No matter what her age, most women find big band music terribly romantic, so you may want to scare up some Glenn Miller tunes. This idea scores a 10 in Truly Sappy Romance but trust me, she'll eat it up with a spoon.

7. If you have a pool (or access to a private one), have yourself some laughs one night and try making love on an inflatable pool chair. You know, the ones you see sun-bludgeoned, half-conscious folks drifting by on? It's a real challenge, full of comedic—but romantic!—potential.

8. Can't afford to go to Hawaii? Try using a little imagination instead. A couple of flowered shirts, a few leis, a little Hawaiian music and—*voila!* Serve drinks in halved coconut shells. Roast pork on the barbecue. Hang a paper moon in the living room or get a tape of waves crashing on the sand. One determined gentleman I know lay a tarp down in his bedroom, poured sand on the tarp, tacked tinfoil waves to the wall, and hung a single moon-shaped paper lantern over the bed. He cleaned it up later, too! He claims it was the closest he's ever going to come to having sex on the beach.

9. Even something like a strategically placed picnic can lead to a wild encounter. Pack a lunch and head for

the hills. Or anywhere less frequented. The idea is to "fool around in nature," so privacy is obviously a must. And be sure to include a blanket or a sheet. Otherwise, whoever's on the bottom is going to get dirty.

10. Doing any of the sweet spontaneous activities of our early youth will get her in a playful state of mind. Take her for a surprise trip to the playground, for instance. Push her on the swing, play with her on the teeter-totter. Do the slide. Around sunset public playgrounds and parks are often deserted so you'll have the run of the place. And afterward, why not fool around in your car?

11. Sometimes it's necessary to see your lover with new eyes. From a point of innocence. We all get so bogged down in the excesses of modern living, so hypnotized by the mediums of television and movies, that we fail to see beauty right before our very eyes. The best way I know for recovering that freshness (and with it, the way we used to see each other) is by taking . . . an art class! Especially ones that train you to utilize the creative, colorful, and yes, sexual, *right side* of your brain. These classes are almost like zen meditation in their simplicity so don't be intimidated if you feel you have no artistic talent. I've known many a man and woman who thought him- or herself utterly deficient in that area come away with: a) a keener appreciation of what is beautiful about the world (including their partner!) and b) a creditable proficiency in drawing. Give it a try.

12. Instead of taking a bath by candlelight, try taking a bath in complete darkness. Sometimes by not being

able to see something, we experience the essence of it more keenly. Your sense of smell, of touch, will be heightened dramatically. The sloshing of the water. The roughness of your bath towel. The dewy softness of her skin. This is true sensuality.

13. Have you ever been body-painted? It's terrific fun. You can buy face and body paint anywhere party supplies are sold. Clowns use them to face-paint children at birthday parties. Lay out an old sheet and have at it. You can body-paint simultaneously or take turns. The laughs are guaranteed.

14. Have a bizarre sense of humor? Okay, it's time to really test it with: nude Twister. You remember Twister, don't you? It's that full-contact game you can buy where you and a partner (or partners) place your hands and feet on the designated areas of a plastic mat. Only now you're going to play it nude.

15. Strip poker. When's the last time you played? This is especially sexy if she wears some of the lingerie you bought her (see "A Gentleman's Guide to Buying Lingerie"). You yourself can don some very brief briefs or that funny underwear that has an elephant head on the crotch or hearts all over or whatever. Surprise her with something she hasn't seen before!

16. Long languishing looks. That's the name of the game when you agree to communicate *with your eyes only*—nothing verbal. Picnic in the living room, for example, letting only the eloquence of your eyes and lips and hands tell her how much you love her.

17. Have you ever shared an ice cream cone? All that sweet, cold, creamy ice cream oozing over your tongue, your fingers, *her* tongue, *her* fingers . . . get my drift? Anyone who's ever seen the movie *Tom Jones* will know what I'm getting at. Food is wonderfully sensual. Eating a particularly succulent fruit can yield the same experiences. Doing sensual things done for sensuality's sake—not necessarily as a prelude to intercourse—is what being a great lover is all about. Remember: it's what you do *when your clothes are on* that will determine your success with women.

18. Lazing around in a hammock is hands-down one of life's finer pleasures. The drone of planes and lawnmowers, the mad inhuman noise, is of no concern to you when you're semi-conscious. But a hammock for two—ah, there's the rub! The challenge is holding her still long enough to make contact (you have a very yielding plane of resistance) so I recommend you straddle the hammock and rock her frontward and backward. And if your backyard affords inquisitive neighbors too many opportunities of seeing you, set your hammock up indoors. The living room, perhaps. These things can be very user-friendly when you get to know them.

19. The next time you're broiling at the beach, the sun beating unmercifully down upon you, buy a drink and fish out a couple of ice cubes. Tell your lover to close her eyes. Then very slowly slide an ice cube down her forehead, across her lips, oozing over the contours of her throat, the curves of her breasts, melting over her stomach, gliding down her legs . . . then starting with another one, slide it up

again. Of course I dare you to remain unaroused during this procedure, so discretion is advised.

20. Where is the place you first met your sweetheart? What a terrific surprise it would be for you to take her there! Of course if you met by locking bumpers on the freeway, that's probably not ideal. In that case, take her to the first place you went on a date. Sometimes we lose sight of all the wonderful feelings we used to have for each other. Recapturing a moment when those feelings were just beginning—well, there's no better way to rekindle those romantic fires! Yes, I even talked to a man who met his wife when he was an inmate in prison. So what do they do most anniversaries? You guessed it. It's a strange world.

21. There's nothing like live music, is there? The only problem is we usually have to go out to see it. And what with the parking, the people, and the jockeying for seats, even diehard romantics have a difficult time getting starry-eyed. That's why you're going to invite the band to your house! Okay, maybe not the Rolling Stones but a nice string quartet would be appropriate. Make dinner for her. If you want, invite some other people on condition that they tactfully withdraw by a specific hour. You'd be surprised at how affordable such goings-on can be.

22. Occasionally I run across a man that all untaught knows how to make a woman happy. Such a one was Carl. And when Carl had differences of opinion with Myrna, his wife of thirty years, he donned a special T-shirt. Oh, Carl certainly stood his guns in an argument. But he never lost sight of what was important: his love for Myrna. Because on this personalized T-shirt was printed all his reasons for loving her—her personality, her sense of humor, a way she had of making anybody feel good about himself (how's "I would have been a priest if I hadn't met Myrna" for personalized?). And nine times out of ten Carl's wearing of the shirt mellowed them both. It crystallized their priorities and made lesser concerns (like toothpaste and toilet seats) unimportant. It's hard for all of us sometimes to see the big picture. Carl just had a particularly creative way of doing so.

23. As Carl demonstrates, getting things in perspective is a must for any couple. But it's tough when the very fact of being a couple makes it challenging to see each other as separate entities. You're always together—walking, sleeping, eating. You rarely have a chance to step back and view the other objectively. That's precisely the problem this idea addresses.

   One night I want you to walk into a romantic restaurant alone and take a table. A few minutes later your lover walks in and takes a table a little ways down but sits facing you. There is no acknowledgment that you know each other, but after a while your eyes happen to meet. Maybe you send her a drink. Throughout the entire meal you make surreptitious eye contact. Perhaps later you follow her home and, without a word spoken, make ravishing love to her. That'll keep the spark alive!

24. There's no denying that long-distance relationships are on the rise. Dual-career couples find themselves challenged not only to keep the home fires burning but to make enough money to buy the wood! If you,

too, are caught on opposite coasts, send her a surprise ticket. Do it! And when she flies in, take her for a wonderful dinner *à deux* and then a carriage ride in the park. Perhaps a weekend of deluxe accommodations at a swank hotel would tickle her fancy. After all, why even make the sacrifice of being apart if you can't spend the money that justifies your separation?

25. A picture is worth a thousand words, right? So get your camera and start clicking. Create a photo album chronicling the romantic odyssey of your relationship! Start, perhaps, with the place you met (or the place she was born!) and go from there. Don't forget to include pix of places of special significance to you both. Surprise her with it when you're through. Many women are unabashedly sentimental—chances are she'll love it!

26. Now wouldn't it be nice to support the arts *and* give your love life the boost it needs? Every city has its share of unemployed singers and musicians, so get a group together and one night (not too late or your neighbors will call the cops) have them serenade your sweetheart beneath her bedroom window. They don't have to be there for hours; just long enough to get your point across. Won't *you* be the talk of the town!

27. One devilishly suave and cultured European gentleman of my recent acquaintance bought his girlfriend a charm bracelet. Every six months or so he would add to it, presenting the new trinket over dinner with an explanation of why he chose it for her. Blue, for instance, was for the color of her eyes. A small airplane signified the places he wanted to take her. Every charm on it was a gift of love and romance and to this day you couldn't pry that thing off Sue's wrist with a crowbar.

28. Some things are just so perfect they require an audience. And some cities are so big you'll get an audience whether you want one or not. New York is one of those. So the next time you and your honey visit the Big Apple (or any city where public transportation is readily available), meet like strangers on the train. Or the subway. Or a cab. Make eye contact. Sit too close. You can even pass a note or two. Cabs especially lend themselves to this kind of encounter. Make the most of it!

29. Keeping in mind the fact that most women love public avowals of your affection, send a box of fortune cookies to her at the office. Inside each cookie will be slips of paper attesting to your undying devotion. "I adore you" is appropriate but don't be afraid to go out on a limb with "Tonight, my sweet, I will eat you like you eat this cookie." But make sure she doesn't share them with co-workers! Be outrageous! Have fun! Romance is not for the weak of heart.

30. Romeo said, "Two of the fairest stars in all the heaven/Having some business, do entreat her eyes/To twinkle in their spheres till they return." And that's just what you're going to do to show how much you care. At Star Registry, phone 800-468-4410, fax 206-485-2749, you can name an actual star after your sweetheart. They'll send her a certificate and everything. Now who can beat that for romantic?

31. This one takes some planning (and not a small amount of money) but boy oh boy does this have a devastating effect on the ladies! You'll need to start at a major department store. Pick five outfits you think your lover will like, leave your credit card number with the salesperson, and send a note to your lover at work telling her she's got a surprise awaiting her at ____ department store. Once she arrives, the salesperson will tell her she is permitted to choose one of the five outfits. Then, after making her selection, she is instructed to choose matching shoes in the shoe department and an accessory. Once her wardrobe is completed, she is to meet you at a certain restaurant where you await with a bottle of champagne. Gosh, do you think there's any possibility she'll be giddy with delight? And you, you lucky dog, will be the recipient of all her beauty and gratitude!

32. Yet some of us are a few dollars shy of our first million so for those who smoke exotic dreams in small pipes, let me suggest this: wash her hair. That's right, get in the shower with her (or the bath) and wash her luxurious tresses. For there are few things more sensual than having a lover wash your hair. Do it slowly, with lots of shampoo. Comb through the creme rinse. Douse her with warm water. Really spend your time with it and sometime later she'll be encouraged to reciprocate. No need for conversation—just let your fingers do the talking!

33. Sometimes we overlook the obvious by forgetting to ingratiate ourselves with our Significant Other's mother. May I suggest a dozen roses? Send them with a note thanking her for having a girl—the woman of your dreams. This is especially wise if you anticipate a *serious* long-term relationship. Harmonious relations with a potential mother-in-law are an investment in your future, amigo! And after she finds out how sweet you were to her mother, she might do something her mother wouldn't approve of to you!

34. A delightful way to signify a budding commitment is to lay out a new terrycloth robe, soap, toothbrush and toothpaste, and other personal sundries on the bed for her. To make these items available after her shower, say, would be truly and splendidly romantic. It's this kind of thoughtfulness that will set you apart from the herd of her other suitors, or keep you out of the divorce courts.

35. A huge number of Americans speak English as a foreign language not to mention the countless others who speak languages other than English. Are you one of them? If so, speak with the tongue of angels! She doesn't have to speak Farsi to understand you when you whisper something foreign in her ear, between ecstatic cries and groaning curses. French, Italian, Chinese, you name it. Just keep your voice rich with expression!

36. A surprising number of women find the sight of men masturbating (*only* men they know and love, thank you) to be wildly erotic. A fair number of men find the sight of women masturbating erotic, too. Therefore, should the opportunity present itself, suggest she pretend you're not there and see what she does to please herself. This is especially sexy if there's a door separating you and you peek through a keyhole (makes her feel less self-conscious, too), or a glass door, or at the very least a sheer fabric like mosquito netting hung around the bed.

37. Since surprise is a key element in being wildly romantic and sexy, fix her a sack lunch tomorrow and slip a love note in with her sandwich. She'll love it! It can be something as simple as "I love you" or a detailed explanation of what you're going to do to her later. She'll have all day at work to ruminate on the scenario you've presented and won't she be in a good mood come five o'clock! And you, you romantic rascal you, will stand alone as being THE sexiest, sweetest guy on the planet!

38. Have you ever started an accordion story? All you need is a piece of paper, a pen, an imagination, and a sense of humor. At the top of the page, write two or three lines describing one of many ways you want to drive her wild, leaving your last sentence open (i.e. "So then I took you . . ."). Now fold the paper over so all she sees is the last sentence. Without peeking, she has to continue the story, folding the paper over once again when she's through. Now it's your turn to continue. Once you've filled the entire page, unfold the "accordion" and read the story together. It's a blast! And so, so funny.

39. The fact is few men use the full potential of their penises. They don't move as enthusiastically as women wish. So next time, pull out almost all the way until just the head of your penis is still inside of her before plunging in again. Or . . . penetrate as far as you can go, moving deeply within her. Ideally, you might alternate. The trick is to vary your move-

ments and to maximize your size. And few things are sexier than a man truly enjoying his own sexuality.

40. Many cities boasting harbors or lakes have paddleboats you can rent. Paddleboats are small fiberglass conveyances that have pedals for your feet. They hold two or at the most four and you get to churn around the harbor feeling the wind on your face. They're enormous fun and for your purposes anyway, wildly romantic! So grab your sweetheart and head on down to the paddleboats because once you're in the middle of the water, you should kiss her romantically, whisper sweet nothings, ask her to marry you—whatever! It'll be a day she remembers, I promise you!

41. When two people have been married a long time, sex has long since become a given in the relationship. Not necessarily so! One of the most effective ways of keeping the spark alive is by agreeing to kiss passionately for a weekend without going any further. The next few days you only pet. The weekend after that you perform oral sex on each other but no intercourse. And so on. It is the prohibition that rekindles the flames, that gets you itchy for each other again. Only when you can't stand it anymore do you finally indulge your newfound passion for each other. But proceed slowly. The idea is to prolong your delights.

42. Without starting a major conflagration, move all available candles into one room (the bedroom, for instance), buy a dozen more, and light them all. Few things look more romantic, sexy, and appealing than twenty or so candles (fifty if you have them!) flickering in the darkness. They make satin sheets positively gleam and every woman knows she looks terrific by candlelight. Purchase a couple of candelabras or the kinds of candles that float like lilies in a basin of water. Be creative and imaginative—she'll love you for it!

43. One of the sexiest things you can do then is to eat her out, make love, eat her out, make love, and then when you're ready to come, let go all over her breasts or in her mouth or wherever else your fancies take you! By varying your activity you keep her guessing as to what you're going to do next and *that*, my friends, will drive her wild indeed!

44. There are so many things you can do to heighten a woman's pleasure it boggles the mind. Surprising then how few of them a mediocre lover will discover in his lifetime! One of the wildest erogenous zones on a woman's body is the back of her neck. The *nape* of her neck. And if you were to bite it vigorously but not painfully, especially that little dip beneath her hairline, it would certainly go a long way toward making you a Master of the Unexpected. The same thing goes for biting her buttocks. Or between her thighs. Biting is sexy providing it's done right—gently.

45. The next time it rains, instead of going fishing, set that tent up in your backyard, roll out the old sleeping bag, and invite your sweetie on a spontaneous romantic interlude with the sound of the rain on your roof. Bring food, a little wine, maybe a heater if it's cold. Happily, there are no phones, no fax machines, no TVs to make you crazy. Just you, her, and Mother Nature. Ah, *think* of it!

46. Okay, when's the last time you said "I love you"? Hmmm? Maybe last week, quickly and in passing? Maybe two months ago on the phone? Well, if you do love her, there is no more romantic and sexy time to express it than in bed. Especially during orgasm—hers or yours. It's the kind of thing writers of romantic fiction love to detail in their novels. You're never more vulnerable than when you're coming inside a woman so why not go the extra mile and let her know?

47. What more playful way to suggest something naughty than writing it on the roll of paper towels in the kitchen? Well, maybe not if there are kids around but I think you get my drift! She's sure to love it if you write something spicy and next time she'll undoubtedly surprise *you!*

48. Sometimes the call of the wild can happen at the most inopportune times—when you're driving on the freeway, for instance. But why should you let that stop you? I know many couples who pull over on a whim and enjoy a quickie in the back seat. What's an emergency lane for, anyway?

49. Few things feel more exquisitely erotic than having a man perform oral sex on you after having drunk a very hot beverage. Or a very cold one. Perhaps you can vary the temperature, thereby discovering which one she likes best. You will need to keep the drink handy so you can maintain the extreme hotness or coldness but for heaven's sake, don't use ice

cubes directly on her vagina! Most women, in fact, prefer the hot beverage to the cold; the chill tends to numb their full range of sensation.

50. There's nothing like doing something sappy and adolescent to win her heart, so why not call a radio station and have them dedicate a song to your sweetheart? Every couple seems to have "their song"—one that, to them, perfectly epitomizes their feelings for each other. If you don't have one yet, pick one. And watch her heart strings *quiver!*

After Words

Now you know. The secret to driving women wild in bed is not your ability to maintain an erection for ten hours. It's knowing how to touch, to lick, to move; perhaps most of all it's understanding how to set the emotional and psychological stage for your partner. In gaining a woman's sexual trust, you are gaining your sexual freedom. It is remembering that sex is as different for women as our genitalia are different from each other's.

We suffer from a surfeit of illusion. Sex is so perfectly choreographed in the movies—beautiful people doing beautiful things. Fornication to a million-dollar soundtrack. Few of a man's friends have the courage to admit they're not the stallions they pretend to be. It's hard not to feel like you're the only one with doubts, questions, indecision. The whole world seems to burn with erotic fire.

But you're not alone. Everyone feels ill-equipped to handle all the challenges facing couples today. Who to date, where to date, what to do when you date? Keeping the post-nuptial fires alive. Sex after starting a family. Is it any wonder we feel overwhelmed, perhaps even (horrors!) apathetic?

But wisdom is the sludge that's left after you've drained the cup of every embarrassment, mistake, misstep you could possibly drink. So you must continue to learn. To explore. To seek the status of the truly sexually legendary. Read everything you can about women, about sex, about yourself. Study tantric sex, the sociology of sex, sex throughout the ages. And listen. Always listen. We never learn anything by talking.

I leave you with this final piece of advice: passionate encounters start where theory leaves off and action begins. In other words, it's not enough to read about it. You must do it. So roll on your condom and pluck up your confidence because, my dear friend, *you* are about to graduate to the ranks of the sexually legendary.

I applaud you!